GW00320323

VOLUNTEER VOICES

BELFAST'S CREATIVE EXTREMISTS

ISBN: 978-0-9566082-0-8

Published by Voluntary Service Bureau, © 2010

Printed by GPS Colour Graphics Ltd, Belfast

Voluntary Service Bureau
34 Shaftesbury Square
Belfast
BT2 7DB

Tel: 028 9020 0850
Fax: 028 9020 0860
Email: info@vsb.org.uk
Web: www.vsb.org.uk

LOTTERY FUNDED

CHANGING LIVES
THROUGH VOLUNTEERING

CONTENTS

ACKNOWLEDGEMENTS

Volunteer Voices – Belfast's Creative Extremists is the product of an exciting and enjoyable two year oral and social history project supported by the Heritage Lottery Fund. Our thanks to the Heritage Lottery Fund for sharing our vision for the project, its active involvement and providing the resources to enable us to capture the volunteer stories of Belfast – stories which give a voice to the immense and significant contribution made by people not because they have to, but because they want to. It has been a privilege and often a humbling experience for all of us involved with the *Volunteer Voices* project to listen to their stories. Over 110 individuals agreed to tell their story. Saying "Thank you for your participation" is somewhat trite and does not fully reflect the inspiration and powerful contribution you collectively have given to the making of a good society.

Unfortunately not all the stories can be accommodated within the book; however all the stories have already been archived at VSB.

Early in the project two groups of volunteers stepped forward to assist and, as only volunteers can do, their involvement brought the concept to life. The advice, knowledge and skills of the Expert Advisory Panel were invaluable. We deeply appreciate the wisdom shared and given by: Brian Turner, Maggie Andrews, Wendy Osborne, Kate Campbell, Will Glendinning, Peter Graham, Mary Hegarty, Robert Heslip and Fionnuala Jay-O'Boyle.

The second group of active volunteers included Margueritte Campbell, Joanne Dunn, Claire Goodwin, Fiona McLaughlin, Harry Press and Julie Anne Young. They undertook training in interview techniques, carried out interviews and followed up on leads. We thank you for your enthusiasm and commitment to the project.

ADVISORY PANEL

Dr Brian Turner
Maggie Andrews
Wendy Osborne
Kate Campbell
Will Glendinning
Peter Graham
Mary Hegarty
Robert Heslip
Fionnuala Jay-O'Boyle.

VOLUNTEERS

Margueritte Campbell
Joanne Dunn
Claire Goodwin
Fiona McLaughlin
Harry Press
Julie Anne Young.

As the project came to life two significant organisations – Belfast City Council and BBC Northern Ireland – offered much needed technical assistance and resources, specialist heritage advice, publicity, interview training and time of personnel to get involved. We would particularly like to thank: Robert Heslip, Heritage Officer, Belfast City Council, for the loan of recording equipment and his advice on archiving and Mark Adair, Head of Corporate and Community Affairs, BBC Northern Ireland, who has taken the *Volunteer Voices* concept and developed a Northern Ireland wide Volunteer Stories section for the BBC Community Bus website. We enjoyed the two days that the bus visited VSB and for the opportunity to be given training in interviewing and editing techniques from Aoife McKevitt and Campbell Lawley. For showing patience, sharing your skills and making it a fun learning experience – thank you.

The publication contains some wonderful photographs, newspaper articles, old programmes / brochures and other memorabilia and we appreciate the contribution by all who searched through their attics and photograph albums to supply this material. We would particularly like to acknowledge Stanley and Mo Matchett for providing access to Stanley's extensive collection of photographs. As a professional photographer for over 40 years, Stanley has captured significant moments in time and we are honoured to include these in this publication to visually bring to life the context in which our creative extremist stories are set. The photographs taken by the late Brian Green, were given to us by Caroline Magowan. Brian was a community activist who lived in the Lower Ormeau Road. His photographs portray the challenges that local people faced but also their resilience and the willingness of people to work for a good society. Many thanks Caroline Magowan for allowing us to use Brian's photographs. Thank you to Wheelworks for allowing use of its image on the 'brickwork' pages.

Finally Jacqui McDowell Hale and Bill Osborne would like to pay tribute to the contribution made by Julie Williams-Nash. Julie was appointed as the part-time co-ordinator of the project but she was much more than that. She became the good parent of *Volunteer Voices*, always available, answering all the demands, finding the resources, preparing agendas, taking notes, carrying out interviews, providing the proofs, hunting down photographs and contributors. Thank you Julie for the self-effacing manner in which you carried out this pivotal parental role.

Bill Osborne – Director, VSB
Jacqui McDowell Hale – Head of Operations, VSB

This book is dedicated to the memory of two energetic and inspirational creative extremists,

Peter McLachlan and Sydney Stewart

Peter and Sydney were active, overtly and covertly, in local politics, totally dedicated to peace and reconciliation, passionate in their resolve to overcome disadvantage, and both had a strong personal commitment to social justice.

For many years they were Chief Officers of two of Belfast's well known charities, Sydney with Voluntary Service Belfast and Peter with Bryson House. In these roles they were archetypal social entrepreneurs and renowned mavericks, always seeking solutions – "No" was not a word they heard or understood when it came to finding solutions to problems. Driven by the desire to make life better for all, they never flinched when it came to using their vast network of contacts for information, resources, influence and most of all getting you committed to action.

Their energy, enthusiasm and commitment was infectious and daunting. Sadly both died at relatively young ages, Sydney in 1987 at the age of 50 and Peter in 1999 aged 63. Their legacy is seen in the lives of individuals they inspired or helped and in the work of many organisations they established, supported and developed. Their stories encourage us all to go that extra mile, in the words of Seamus Heaney to,

" yearn for hammerblows on clinkered planks,
the uncompromised report of driven thole-pins,
to know there is one amongst us who never swerved
from all his instincts told him was right action,
who stood his ground in the indicative,
whose boat will lift when the cloudburst happens."

(From The Canton of Expectations)

FOREWORD

Most of the past forty years of Belfast's history has been turbulent, fractured and painful. The City suffered and over 1,500 of its people died; countless others injured. During the early 1970's Belfast experienced one of the largest movements of population in Europe since the Second World War. Later with the erection of 'peace walls' and interface barriers, it became, and still is, a physically divided city. Neil Jarman in *Security and Segregation, Interface Barriers in Belfast* has identified "83 barriers, mainly in clusters, in 14 areas of the City."

Amidst this reality, however, are countless stories of people with hope. People equipped with enthusiasm and energy who gave their time as volunteers. Using whatever skills they had and picking up more on the way, they travelled into "the valley of beasts and monsters" and "faced the dragon's fire" believing it was possible to make a difference.

On the night of the 2009 USA Presidential Election Barack Obama said that "while we breathe, we hope, and where we are met with cynicism and doubt, and those who tell us that we can't, we will respond with that timeless creed that sums up the spirit of people: yes we can."

Belfast volunteers with their 'yes we can' attitude, hope, endurance, commitment and actions have left a significant imprint on their own lives, the lives of others and on the life of the City. They are the most unlikely of heroes, often reluctant to accept any form of reward or recognition. Without their engagement and contribution to holding the fabric of society together one wonders how The Agreement and Peace Process, through all its false beginnings and stumbling, would have endured. Indeed they are the crying head and hand holding the still burning lamp in Picasso's "Guernica", symbolic of the hope and spirit of people amidst disorder, despair and fear.

Volunteer Voices – Belfast's Creative Extremists is a collection of Belfast's volunteers' stories told in their own words, reflecting humility, generosity of spirit and the sheer perseverance of people. They display a rich and colourful tapestry of civic engagement despite the backdrop of conflict and despair, depicting people who believe in the possible, who build new realities for themselves and others.

The stories are accompanied by four personal reflections from Gerald Dawe, Poet, Fionnuala O'Connor, Journalist, Sir Kenneth Bloomfield, retired Head of Civil Service and Victims Commissioner, and Duncan Morrow, Director of the Community Relations Commission.

Alongside Belfast's history of conflict and rebellion is another face, often forgotten, of radicalism, social activism and philanthropy. Jonathon Bardon's introduction is an insightful perspective into this aspect of Belfast life and provides the historical context and foundations for today's civil society.

Through this *Volunteer Voices* project VSB aimed to capture a part of the past that we believe is a significant aspect of the social history of Belfast. The life and heartbeat of the city is after all its people.

Bill Osborne, 2010

Belfast in 1690

A PERSPECTIVE ON THE GENESIS OF SOCIAL ACTIVISM IN BELFAST

Jonathan Bardon

Until the end of the twelfth century Belfast was merely a crossing place where travellers made their way over sandbanks exposed at low tide, across the estuary of the River Lagan, at the point where the Farset stream joined it. Then in 1177 the Norman adventurer, John de Courcy, invaded Ulster with twenty-two knights and some three hundred foot soldiers and conquered the coastlands of the present counties of Antrim and Down. Carrickfergus and Downpatrick emerged as the principal towns in what became the Earldom of Ulster and Belfast was no more than a village clustered around a modest castle guarding the crossing.

The Earldom was on the margins of the Lordship of Ireland, the territory controlled by the English Crown. From early in the fourteenth century, Gaelic lords from central Ulster overwhelmed the Earldom and it was not until the close of Elizabeth's reign in 1603 that the English Crown was in full control. Elizabeth granted Belfast and the territory surrounding it to one of her most successful

commanders, Sir Arthur Chichester. Chichester, appointed the royal governor of Ireland by James I, became the principal architect of the Plantation of Ulster. He was determined to set a good example to fellow colonists by promoting the development of Belfast, ordering the firing of over a million bricks and building a Jacobean mansion, Belfast Castle, in the vicinity of today's Castle Place.

Seventeenth-century Belfast was almost entirely a planters' town. Chichester obtained a charter for it in 1613: he was 'Lord of the Castle' and appointed all thirteen members of the town's corporation and they in turn elected two members to sit in the Irish Parliament. When Chichester died his property was inherited by his brother Edward who became the first Earl of Donegall (the title is explained by Sir Arthur's acquisition of almost the entire peninsula of Inishowen in north Donegal). Belfast was extremely fortunate to escape destruction in a century when Ulster was periodically convulsed by rebellion, massacres and rampaging armies. The town was besieged briefly by Cromwell's forces but it prospered in the quiet years after the restoration of Charles

II in 1660. Much of Ulster's surplus agricultural produce was brought there to be shipped across the Irish Sea and to France and Spain. Though Belfast was still small by comparison with southern cities, such as Cork, Limerick, Galway and Waterford, it became the most flourishing port in Ulster. Sometime before 1662 Belfast acquired the right to collect its own customs and this encouraged the use of the port. In 1685, 247 vessels entered Belfast, 82 of them based in the town totalling 3,228 tons. The colonists there, knowing the distaste people across the Irish Sea had for Irish butter, catered for British taste, and made Belfast, along with Youghal in Co. Cork, one of the principal suppliers of butter to England. Tanned leather, skins, beef, tallow, salmon, wool and linen were also important exports. In turn Ulster's growing demand for port and exotic colonial products was catered for by cargoes landed at full tide at what is now the bottom of High Street. In 1683 the American colonies exported 382,640 lbs of tobacco to the town.[1]

The town's government was placed firmly in the hands of the Chichester family. The Earl of Donegall chose the 'Sovereign' (the town mayor) and the twelve other free burgesses who were to draft the laws of the town with the advice and

consent of the Earl. The minutes of the corporation survive and show that the council was primarily concerned to regulate the markets and activities such as brewing, and to ensure that malt kilns did not set the town on fire.[2] Although prosperous and growing, not all of Belfast's population lived like their lords and masters. Unlike England, with its system of parish relief established by law during the reign of Elizabeth, Ireland's destitute lacked a safety net which was backed by legislation and public funding.

Prosperity depended not only on trade cycles but to a very great extent on the harvest. A string of harvest failures in the 1690s brought about such a terrible famine in Scotland that perhaps one quarter of the population died there with many of the survivors fleeing to Ulster to make a fresh start. In Ulster many starved during the scarcities of 1726-29. Then in 1739-40 arctic conditions followed by a long drought resulted in a terrible famine, at its most severe in Ulster, in 1741. The Irish called this bliadhain an áir, year of the slaughter; around 300,000 died, a death toll in proportion as terrible as the Great Famine a century later.[3] Clearly there was a need for volunteering and charitable works.

Belfast's earliest record of a charitable contribution can be read on the Subscription Board in Clifton House Boardroom: 'Edward Holmes, burgess, died in June 1631 and left to the poor decayed inhabitants of Belfast 40 lib'. £40 was then a very considerable sum and it was this bequest which initiated an unofficial – and ad hoc – system of relief. By an extremely tortuous route, this 'Poores Money' (which had reached a total of £325 by 1675) led to the formation of the Belfast Charitable Society 121 years later. Most Belfast merchants seem to have left money to the poor of the parish. 'These bequests were surprisingly modest', Jean Agnew concludes

Image from *The Town Book of the Corporation of Belfast*, by Robert M Young

in her study of Belfast merchant families in the seventeenth century.[4] Only two other merchants left £40 each: Thomas Waring in 1665 and Hugh Eccles in 1680. Bequests were more often in the region of £5 - £10. William Leathes, Sovereign of Belfast on three occasions, died in 1660 and the Town Book records 'Losse of soe honest just and upright man and eminent in his place being ever a support to ye needy fatherless and widows'. His nephew, John Leathes, who became a Church of Ireland clergyman, gave quarter of his annual income to

Image from The Town Book of the Corporation of Belfast, by Robert M Young

the poor and left them half his goods – though this probably went to the needy in the rural parishes where he served.[5]

Belfast surrendered without a fight to the forces of James II in 1689 and the following year citizens welcomed William III, urging him to 'pull the stiff neck of every Papist down'. Thus Belfast escaped the destruction endured by many other towns, such as Carrickfergus and Newry, during the war which was brought to an end on 12 July 1691 at Aughrim with a Williamite victory. However, the town remained very dependent on the patronage and interest of the Chichesters. Unfortunately this expected support was frequently not forthcoming. In 1705 the 3rd Earl of Donegall had been killed fighting in Spain with the Duke of Marlborough's army, leaving as his successor a weak-minded minor. In 1708 an accidental fire gutted Belfast Castle and three of the new Earl's sisters died in the blaze. Henceforth, the Chichesters were absentee landlords. The incapacity of the 4th Earl, legal wrangling, and the timidity of the trustees ensured that the Chichesters provided

no initiative in improving Belfast. Above all, the development of the town was stifled by short leases and tenancies which carried no obligation to carry out improvements.

The result was that the Corporation did little. It could barely meet the expense of running the market out of customs dues and tolls levied on outsiders. There was not even a town hall or courthouse and by 1664 the Corporation was forced to rent a building for the purpose from George Macartney, the wealthiest man in Belfast and its Sovereign. Even the annual rent of £5 (and the £4 required for a new plush cushion for the town hall) had to be raised by a levy on the inhabitants. Since the Chichester family, the Donegall estate trustees and the Corporation had shirked their duties, it was left to public-spirited citizens to do what they could.

In 1603 Sir Arthur Chichester had planned Belfast as a town for English colonists. Actually most of the incomers were Scots, Presbyterian by religious affiliation. These Presbyterians had a long tradition of standing up to Anglican landlords and rectors and taking the initiative themselves. On Friday 28 August 1752, in a Belfast tavern called The George Inn, on the corner of John Street and North Street, a group of citizens resolved 'to consider of a proper way to raise a sum for building a poor House & Hospital & a new Church in or near the Town of Belfast'. They also agreed to raise funds by selling lottery tickets because 'a Poor House and Hospital are greatly wanted in the Town of Belfast for the support of real objects of charity in this Parish, for the employment of idle beggars that crowd to it from all parts of the North, and for the reception of infirm and diseased poor'.[6]

Raising the money proved difficult (especially as the government declared the first lottery illegal). Finding a suitable site was another problem. Members of the Belfast Charitable Society wrote to Lord Donegall in 1763. The 5th Earl was still a minor and members had to wait three years, shortly after the Earl had reached his majority, to get a reply. The 5th Earl was decidedly more energetic than his predecessors and was to do much to improve Belfast. Lord Donegall granted them 'the Ground on the North West side of the Road leading to Carrickfergus fronting the New Street' – much of which the Society still possesses. In the end the Poor House (now known as Clifton House) was built largely to the design of one its members, Robert Joy, son of the founder of the Belfast News-Letter, Francis Joy. The foundation stone was laid on 1 August 1771 and Clifton House opened three years later in 1774.

Clifton House was to be the principal focus for volunteer work in Belfast for many years to come. Since there was no provision for the levying of a poor rate, the business of raising the necessary cash was left to the generosity of citizens. At the same time the Society had to comply with legislation to detain vagrants (some arrested by the Sovereign's personal servant known as Dudley the Bang-beggar) and issue them with metal badges to permit them to beg. Inmates were given work including spinning, weaving, net making and picking oakum from old ropes known as 'junk'. Meals provided included 'bread cheese and milk', 'buttermilk, stirabout and butter', 'rice, porridge' and 'pease porridge' – good fare in a country where so many people subsisted on an unrelieved diet of potatoes and buttermilk. Gifts supplemented the diet: sacks of potatoes sent in by the local gentry; butter condemned for false weight sent up by the Sovereign; and necks and haughs of beef from Waddell Cunningham, then Belfast's most prosperous merchant.[7]

Children made up a high proportion of the inmates. Physicians seem to have given their services without charge. Dr William Drennan (the man who coined the term 'The Emerald Isle' and later the real founder of the Society of United Irishmen and of the Belfast Academical Institution) gave a lecture before the board 'setting forth the utility of a mode of inoculation being introduced into this House' and thus took a lead in pioneering cowpox

Clifton House, Belfast

inoculation against smallpox in his home town. Robert Joy was particularly concerned that the children be taught a trade. In 1777, during a severe economic downturn as the American War raged, Joy toured parts of England and Scotland in what was, in effect, an audacious exercise in industrial espionage. He brought back spinning machines and set them up in the Poor House. He was playing a key role in making Belfast a cradle

Image from *The Town Book of the Corporation of Belfast, by Robert M Young*

of the industrial revolution. Joy – in partnership with watchmaker Thomas McCabe and sea captain John McCracken – set up Belfast's first cotton mill in Francis Street with machinery 'to spin twist by water in the manner of Richard Arkwright'. Many of those employed were children from the Poor House.

Along with cargoes of sugar, tobacco and other goods from overseas brought in to Donegall Quay came new ideas from Scotland, France and America. The Enlightenment took deep root in Belfast and during the late eighteenth century the Presbyterians there made Belfast the most radical town in the island. In a dramatic demonstration of their support for Catholic claims to full emancipation, the Volunteers there formally admitted Catholics to their ranks in May 1784. They raised most of the funds needed to build the first Catholic chapel in the town, St Mary's, and paraded in full dress uniform and marched to Mass when the building was completed.

Some radicals became revolutionaries. In 1798 Belfast became the second largest garrison in Ireland and troops – largely billeted in the White

Linen Hall, now the site of the City Hall – marched out to crush the Presbyterian insurgents at Antrim and Ballynahinch in June. The rebel leader, Henry Joy McCracken (son of Captain John McCracken), was hanged at Cornmarket in July.[8] His sister, Mary Ann, who had also been up to her neck in subversive activities, was to spend most of the rest of her long life as the dynamic secretary of the Ladies Committee in the Poor House.[9] Other United Irishmen in the town who had survived were thankful they had not been transported, imprisoned or hanged. They now threw themselves into business activity and, generally avoiding politics, they devoted much of their free time to promoting the welfare of fellow citizens less fortunate than themselves. In any case, most radically-minded inhabitants of Belfast had been opposed to violent revolution, however much they despised those who wielded power. The Protestants of Belfast, unlike those of Dublin and those who were members of Orange lodges particularly west of the River Bann, welcomed the Act of Union of 1800 if only because it seemed to bring to an end the rule of a narrow oligarchy of Anglican landlords, lawyers, clergy and their relatives, the 'Protestant Ascendancy'.

During the 1790s, in addition to work undertaken in the Charitable Society, public-spirited citizens had set up: the General Dispensary, 1792; the Lying-in Hospital, 1794; the Union School (for the maintenance and education of destitute girls), 1795; and the first fever hospital, 1797.[10] The need for volunteering certainly increased in the following century: Belfast had good claim to be the fastest-growing urban centre of the United Kingdom in the nineteenth century. Stimulated by demand during the Napoleonic Wars, the town's cotton mills firmly established Belfast as Ireland's most important industrial centre. Tall mills spinning linen yarn by water and steam power began to rise up from the late 1820s. The technical problems of weaving flax by power were overcome in the 1850s and by the middle 1860s the town had become the greatest centre of linen production in the world. An indigenous engineering industry evolved to feed the needs of linen concerns. The dredging of the Victoria Channel to enable large vessels to come up to Belfast at any tide not only stimulated trade but also created an artificial island, Queen's Island, next to Short Strand – this became the unlikely location for iron and steel shipbuilding. By the 1880s Harland and Wolff had become the largest shipbuilding firm in the world.

Industrial and commercial success drew in to the town tens of thousands from the impoverished and heavily-populated Ulster countryside. The population of Belfast increased by almost 47 per cent between 1801, when it was 19,000, and 1811, when it was 27,832. In 1841 it was 70,447; in 1871, 174, 412; and by 1901 it was 349,180, the largest city in Ireland. Rather late in the day, Belfast won recognition as a city in 1888. The great majority of citizens for most of the century had not been born in Belfast and the accent

New Seal of the City of Belfast. 1890.

changed from one similar to that in Ballymena to one strongly influenced by that of Co. Armagh. Catholics, in the previous century an insignificant proportion of the population, formed 32 per cent of the population by 1834 and though the percentage fell to 25 by 1901 their numbers increased – there were more Catholics then in Belfast than in the county of Fermanagh where they formed a majority. Immigrants, both Protestant and Catholic, brought with them their ancient loyalties, fears and prejudices and chose where they settled in Belfast with care. Along the shifting frontiers of Protestant and Catholic enclaves fierce sectarian battles raged, periodically inflamed by the debate on Ireland's political future.[11]

For the first forty years of the nineteenth century those with responsibility for governing Belfast proved themselves utterly incapable of rising to the challenge of meeting the needs of such a rapidly growing town. In 1799 the 5th Earl of Donegall, who had become the 1st Marquess of Donegall eight years earlier, died. Though he had done much to improve Belfast, the Marquess had diverted a great deal of his rent income to his new home of Fisherwick Park in Staffordshire. His son and heir, George Augustus, acquired such enormous debts that he had languished in a debtor's prison for a time. On succeeding his father as the 2nd Marquess, he had no choice but to sell nearly all of his property in Belfast – in the form of perpetual leases – and was forced to stay in Ireland living in a modest house in Donegall Place and later in Ormeau Park.

The Corporation was so inattentive to its duties that publicly-minded citizens had to step in. A Voluntary Night Watch operated in 1812 and again in 1816.[12] Volunteers were also responsible for setting up: a Blind

Asylum, 1801; the House of Industry, 1809; the House of Correction, 1817; and the Female Society for Clothing the Poor, 1820. Education was not yet considered the responsibility of governing authorities and, in addition to setting up secondary schools largely for their own benefit, the town's middle class citizens raised funds and organised schools for the poor including the Lancasterian School (in which those taught in turn taught those younger than themselves) off York Street in 1811; the new Sunday School Society (since young people worked six days a week, education had to be provided on Sundays)in the same year; the Brown Street Sunday, Daily and Infant School in 1812; the Sabbath School Union in 1821; the Mechanics Institute (the nucleus of further education in the town) in 1825; and Donegall Street (Catholic) School in 1829.

The Corporation could not even ensure a water supply to the town. Here the Belfast Charitable Society had to take action. By the late eighteenth century the water flowing down the Farset and Blackstaff streams had become so polluted that it could not be used for drinking. In 1778 the Society decided not only to ensure its own pure supply, but also to make a surplus available in times of need. 'We are authorised to mention', the Belfast News-Letter reported on 13 December 1791, 'that a car goes round the town every day with Poor-house water for sale, at the rate of a halfpenny per measure of four gallons; and that the Poor-house Committee will fir up several cars for the purpose in case they find a sufficient demand'. Clearly this was a stop-gap measure. In 1795 the Society leased the Fountainville spring and Monday's Well in the Blackstaff Loney (later the Donegall Road). This was reckoned to yield just over 63 gallons per minute in dry weather. Meanwhile the Society was spending £2,000 buying elm pipes from England and borrowed another £2,000 to continue channelling water to a reservoir in Fountain Street. Eventually it was agreed to develop new supplies from Lyster's Dam at the Malone springs to Stranmillis to connect with the Fountainville water. In 1817 legislation enabled the Society to appoint the Spring Water Commissioners with powers to increase the water rate. By the time an independent Water Board was appointed in 1840, the Society had spent some £30,000. There is little doubt that the citizens of Belfast, and the poor in particular, had benefited greatly from the efforts of the Society to supply the town with pure water.[13]

Citizens were particularly energetic in attempting to improve public health and in providing medical services. The Belfast Medical Society was formed in 1806 and, though it was dissolved in 1814, it was reconstituted in 1822. During a fever epidemic in 1817 the Belfast General Hospital opened in Frederick Street and the Society for the Relief of the Destitute Sick followed in 1826. The first patient for the Lying-in Hospital (number 25 Donegall Street, rented for twelve guineas a year) was admitted in 1799. After moving for a time to Lancaster Street, a handsome building was erected on the Antrim Road and opened in August 1830. It could take eighteen patients only: 'Eligible patients are admitted on presenting a written recommendation of a subscriber, accompanied by a certificate of a respectable householder, as to the fact of her marriage; the recommendation to be countersigned by a member of the Committee. On leaving the hospital, a supply of clothes for the infant is granted'.[14]

'In the autumn of 1830', Dr Andrew Malcolm wrote, 'intelligence reached these shores, that the Asiatic Cholera had crossed the Russian frontier, and was steadily marching in a westward direction...and on the 29th of February, 1832, the first case in this town appeared'.[15] An extremely well coordinated relief scheme was promptly put into action. A Board of Health 'endeavoured, and with great success, to arouse the different authorities in the town, with a view to set everything in order, and to strengthen all the defences in proper time'. Streets and lanes were scrupulously cleaned and 'steps were taken to isolate any case, wherever it might occur, on the moment of its discovery'. A sum of £700 was rapidly raised and used to erect temporary cholera wards behind the fever hospital to take up to fifty patients. Houses of the infected were placed under quarantine ' – all ingress or egress being prevented by a guard of sworn constables; the bedding of the sick was burnt – all washing articles scoured, and the house thoroughly cleansed, fumigated, and white-washed'. The epidemic lasted forty-six weeks. The mortality, Dr Malcolm reported, was around 16 per cent ' – a proportion which contrasted most favourably with the returns from all other towns of similar magnitude'.[16]

In January 1801 the United Kingdom had come into being and Westminster now legislated for Ireland. However, the island continued to be regarded as a country which needed special treatment. A separate administration remained in Dublin Castle with its own civil service. Thought to be especially lawless, Ireland enjoyed ordinary law for only five out of the first fifty years of the Union – for the rest of the time 'coercion' (special powers involving the suspension of habeas corpus) was in operation. At the same time the government was prepared to take on responsibilities they would not think of accepting on the other side of the Irish Sea. Ireland was being used as a social laboratory for trying out national education, publicly funded hospitals, independent policing, unemployment relief schemes, and the like, long before these improvements were introduced into the rest of the United Kingdom.

The New Poor Law of 1834 was extended with some changes to Ireland in 1838. For the first time the island had a national system of poor relief funded by a poor rate. Parishes had to unite into 'unions', each one to erect a workhouse for the destitute. The Belfast Union Workhouse, opened on 11 May 1841 on the Lisburn Road, designed to accommodate 1,000 inmates, was one of the largest and best-equipped in Ireland. Stringent conditions for admission and the harsh regime inside, however, ensured that volunteer work to help the poor was still desperately needed. Once the workhouse opened, the problem of concentrated street begging was much reduced but the institution catered primarily for those largely incapable of earning a living. The workhouse was not suitable for those made redundant during economic downturns. Those temporarily out of work could not afford to rent accommodation. In addition, the rural poor continued to pour into Belfast seeking work. A letter to the Northern Whig on 7 January 1841 observed that the 'extensive manufactories in town induce thousands of poor persons to come annually to Belfast to seek employment; failing to procure this their condition becomes one of the utmost destitution...I have seen groups of these unfortunate wretches huddled together, on the most inclement nights in Smithfield Market-house – certainly as comfortless a resting-place as could be chosen. Persons in this destitute situation, are, now and then, tempted into the commission of trivial offences, to obtain a night's shelter in the Police Office'. He explained that he was accosted in William

Royal Arms, engraved by JAMES SMITH, *circa* 1815.

Street South with the extraordinary request: 'Will you permit me, Sir, to knock you down?' If he 'would be charitable enough to give me in charge to a watchman, for an assault, I would be sure of a night's lodging'.[17]

The editor of the Northern Whig called for a night asylum for the homeless poor and on 12 January 1841 a public meeting agreed to fund such a refuge. The Night Asylum was opened in rented property in Poultry Square in December with accommodation for eighty persons in two dormitories. The facilities were so basic that there were no blankets or beds and the only cooking which could be done was the roasting of potatoes in the fire. Money was raised to keep the place going by subscriptions and by a panorama of local and foreign views in the Exchange Rooms in February 1843. The asylum was taken over by the authorities in 1847 – a year when the Great Famine was at its worst.[18]

The potato blight first struck during the summer of 1845 but it was not until the following year that the entire island was afflicted. Contrary to the popular view, Ulster was hard hit, suffering more than the province of Leinster. Belfast's very prosperity made the town a magnet for those who had nothing. Now that their basic food had been reduced to a blackened, rotting mass by blight, thousands streamed along the roads to Belfast. 'The physical strength of a whole people was reduced', Dr Malcolm recorded, 'and this condition, highly favourable to the plague-breath, resulted in the most terrible epidemic that this island ever experienced'. The Belfast Workhouse, previously shunned by the poor, rapidly filled up. The Fever Hospital was 'so overcrowded that many cases requiring medical and surgical treatment were refused admission'. The Workhouse Board of Guardians, in its minutes of 20 October 1846, observed that 'the alarming increase of typhus fever renders it imperative on this board to prepare without delay for the approaching epidemic'.[19] By the spring of 1847 that epidemic was raging in the town, 'in comparison with which all previous epidemics were trivial and insignificant', wrote Dr Malcolm.

Leading citizens set up a Board of Health in May 1847 to attempt to provide accommodation for fever victims. Sheds were put up in the grounds of the Frederick Street Hospital; a hospital was organised at the Academical Institution; and buildings used during the 1832 cholera epidemic were re-opened. Still there were not enough beds. The recorded fever admissions for 1847 in Belfast were 13,678. On 20 July the Belfast News-Letter reported: 'The hospitals are crowded, and every new building is filled to overflowing as soon as completed. Yet hundreds – for whom there remains no provision – are daily exposed in the delirium of this frightful malady, on the streets, or left to die in their filthy and ill-ventilated hovels'.[20] A fund opened on 15 January 1847 raised around £7,000. Charities in the town provided soup for as many as 15,000 a day, mainly from kitchens in York Street and Howard Street. 'This great movement well became the capital of the North', Dr Malcolm concluded enthusiastically. 'It was the crowning act in her History, and made her, for a time, an example for the world'.[21]

The government declared the famine to be at an end in 1848 but it continued to reap a grim harvest for the next three years. And to add to the misery cholera returned at the end of 1848. The Belfast Sanitary Committee was prepared well in advance and sent out Heath Visitors to advise the poor on how best to avoid the disease. Even so, at the dispensary station alone, 2,282 cases of cholera were recorded in 1849; 997 of these cases died, indicating a death-rate of 33 per cent. Meanwhile citizens set up a Day Asylum in April 1847 in a former iron foundry at May's Dock, Poultry Square, to take in vagrants and to rescue children begging in the streets. This was partly to remove an eyesore from the town but creditable efforts were made to teach children to read and write. The destitute thronged the building to be let in. There were around 46,000 attendances between April and July by people who were fed and cleansed, including 11,500 girls who were taught the use of a needle and 11,000 boys who were taught 'to use their hands'. Then the work

View of Shankill graveyard, Hogg Collection, courtesy of Belfast City Council.

was taken over by the Poor Law Guardians and by 1849 it had been closed.[22]

Three funds were set up in Belfast to help relieve the sufferings of Famine victims in the south and the west of the island: the Belfast General Relief Fund, the Ladies' Association for the Relief of Irish Distress and the Fund for the Temporal Relief of the Suffering Poor through the Instrumentality of the Clergy of the Established Church. At first the Catholic Bishop of Down and Connor, Dr Cornelius Denvir, was involved but he appears to have been sidelined by those Protestants who could not resist the opportunity charitable assistance gave for a bit of proselytism.

Though Ireland made a remarkable recovery after the Famine, the rural poor continued to stream into Belfast – those without the resources to move on across the Irish Sea or over to America stayed to eke out miserable existences in the overcrowded and insanitary courts and entries of the town.

In 1840, following a damning report by government commissioners, the old unrepresentative Corporation had been swept away and replaced by one elected by ratepayers. The commissioners reported that the old corporation 'confers on the inhabitants no benefit' and listed abuses 'clearly exemplified in the dissipation of the charitable funds intrusted to the management and distribution of the corporation of this borough'.[23] The new corporation rapidly acquired a reputation for being blatantly corrupt and unblinkingly sectarian but it was dynamic – the Conservative majority in the Council (unlike its counterparts across the Irish Sea) showed no hesitation in applying for additional powers to borrow money for widening old streets, building new streets, paving and lighting, laying sewers, and providing fire engines. However, the acquisition of new responsibilities by local government still left many areas of need which could only be met by voluntary action.

A severe downturn in trade caused great distress during the winter of 1857-58. Handloom weavers and stitchers in Ballymacarret (which had become part of Belfast in 1840) were particularly hard hit. Around £300 was collected in subscriptions at a town meeting and eventually £1,035 was raised and used mainly to distribute loaves of bread from the old House of Correction. J. Trueman of the English Bakery gave a hundred four-pound loaves. The relief committee got a contract from the town council to supply 1,000 tons of broken stone which gave work to fifty men. The committee's main activists – John Scott of May Street Foundry, William Spackman of the Northern Clothing Emporium and Mr Carolan of the Ulsterman – were not politicians but they severely criticised the town council for abandoning the destitute. The relief work ended in the summer of 1858.[24]

The entire United Kingdom was plunged into crisis in 1878-79. Tempestuous rain and arctic temperatures added to the misery of trade contraction. This time the mayor, John Browne, and the council, were more active. A Coal Fund was established – but who would give out the fuel? The decision to ask the clergy of the main denominations to supervise distribution inevitably meant that those not connected with churches would be overlooked – 'presumably the undeserving could freeze', Alison Jordan concludes in her history.[25] By mid-January 1879, 778 tons of coal and 4,400 bushels of coke had been given out. Soup was sold at a penny a quart in Ormeau Park and Gloucester Street. Relief work (mainly on park improvements and stone breaking to avoid competing with private enterprise) was provided to the able-bodied – others were expected to get relief within the workhouse. Crowds of men, women and children besieged the town hall offices seeking relief work. A hill on the Falls Road was removed in the relief work which was brought to an end on 22 March.

Meanwhile other citizens had been becoming increasingly concerned with the plight of those suffering physical disabilities, in particular the blind and the deaf (generally described as 'deaf and dumb'). Such people were unable to support themselves

and rarely received religious instruction. In the early nineteenth century money had been raised in Belfast to send such children to the Claremont National Institution for the Education of the Deaf and Dumb at Glasnevin in Dublin. Since fees were twenty guineas a year, it was thought that Belfast should have its own provision. Led by the bookseller, William McComb, citizens formed a committee in 1831 and set up a school in the Independent Chapel in Donegall Street. These premises soon proved to be too confined and, following a major fundraising drive, the county surveyor and architect Charles Lanyon was engaged to design a building on the Lisburn Road. Lord Massereeene and Ferrard opened the much-admired edifice on 24 September 1845. Every pupil had to supply a full set of clothes on being accepted, which must have excluded the very poor.[26]

The regime in the Deaf and Dumb Institute was harsh, even by the standards of the day. Yet much was achieved. The debate (which would go on into the late twentieth century) on whether lip-reading or the use of sign language was best for the deaf had begun. The blind learned to read by a system of raised letters of the alphabet until Braille was introduced in the 1880s. Religious education had an important role and this was of a nature which could only have been acceptable to Protestants. All children had to be given religious instruction in either Church of Ireland or Presbyterian doctrines and attend either St George's parish church or Fisherwick church. The institution set out to prepare pupils to earn a living. The 'deaf and dumb' were taught shoemaking, carpentry, weaving, embroidery and domestic service. It proved more difficult to teach skills to the blind, partly because the mats, baskets and ropes pupils made were difficult to sell. Miss Mary Hobson devoted most of her adult life to preparing the visually impaired for work and was the main driving force behind the establishment of the Belfast Association for the Employment of the Industrious Blind in 1871. Number 6 Howard Street (which then had a large garden) was rented and became Belfast's first workshop for the blind on 19 December 1871.[27] After an uncertain start, the organisation found a dynamic and trustworthy manager in J. H. Hewitt. The main hazard in the making of baskets was fire: the Howard Street building was gutted by fire in 1881 and again in 1883, and new premises in Wellington Street, accidentally burned in 1908, had to be demolished.[28] The organisation, which continued to the 1970s, depended heavily on the earnings of the blind workers but a ladies committee assiduously sought donations and legacies.

At the start of the twentieth century Belfast was one of the most significant arteries of trade and one of the greatest industrial centres in the western world. Certainly its growth had few parallels. The census of 1901 recorded that the number of inhabitants had reached 349,180, the increase for the years 1891 to 1901 alone being over 36 per cent. Though it had been completed only in 1869, the elegant Venetian Gothic Town Hall in Victoria Street was soon considered to be too modest to be the municipal centre. The White Linen Hall in Donegall Square had

been demolished and the new City Hall taking shape behind the hoardings would be an expression of pride in Belfast's achievement in being the port of third importance in the United Kingdom (after London and Liverpool), the biggest city in Ireland with the world's largest shipyard, ropeworks, aerated waters factory, linen mill, tea machinery and fan-making works, handkerchief factory, spiral-guided gasometer, linen machinery works, and tobacco factory.

The chasms that separated the classes widened during the years before the outbreak of the Great War in 1914. Inflationary pressures not matched by rising wages helped to precipitate the Dock Strike which paralysed the city for much of 1907. Atop the social pile there were around three hundred wealthy families, nearly all Protestant, living at Strandtown or on the higher ground on the Malone Road and the Antrim Road. To a remarkable degree these families were interrelated. The men met in boardrooms, at the Harbour Office and the Chamber of Commerce, and dined with each other at the Ulster Club or the Reform Club. At the weekends they sailed on Belfast

Hamill Street area, Hogg Collection, courtesy of Belfast City Council.

Children by a stream at the Shankill Road, Hogg Collection, courtesy of Belfast City Council.

Lough and played golf. Their wives rarely moved out of their social circle but were deeply involved in charitable and Church work. Then, perhaps 6,000 families could afford to employ a maid and be considered members of the middle classes. Voluntary and Church organisations depended heavily on their support and leadership.[29]

A remarkable range of charities provided a crucial service to citizens and absorbed the energies of those with leisure, education and means. Smaller hospitals, such as the Samaritan, 'exclusively devoted to the treatment of diseases peculiar to women', depended entirely on benefactors and on voluntary subscriptions. Inevitably, most of the organisations which absorbed the energies of the middle class were either Catholic or Protestant. They included: the Shankill Road Mission; the Discharged (Protestant Male) Prisoners' Aid Society; Nazareth House; the Ulster Magdalene Society, Donegall Pass; the Presbyterian Orphan Society; the Roman Catholic Ladies' Clothing Society; the Elim Home for Destitute Boys and Girls, 'to rescue orphans,

homeless and destitute street arabs'; the Provident Home for Friendless Females of Good Character, 'who would otherwise be exposed to temptation'; and the Methodists' Belfast Central Mission which – amongst other activities the rest of the year – fed 3,500 every Christmas Day. City fathers and their wives were expected to give their time to be trustees of such funds as Lady Johnson's Bounty (which gave £12 per annum to 'unmarried females, being Protestants, of sober, honest life, above fifty years of age'); the Ulster Children's Aid Society (set up in 1910 'to rescue children from destitution and vagrancy, and from immoral and criminal surroundings'); and Mrs Wilson's Bequest 'to widows of sober, honest life'.[30]

Just over a quarter of male manual workers were skilled artisans (the great majority of them Protestants) earning between 35 and 45 shillings a week and renting parlour terraced houses at five or six shillings a week. They were acutely aware of their privileged position in the working class, which they strove to protect through their trade unions.

Barrack Street National School, Hogg Collection, courtesy of Belfast City Council.

Their work was often dangerous and precarious in times of trade recession. The unskilled – roughly equal numbers of Protestants and Catholics – could expect wages of no more than half those paid to the skilled, and a working week of between sixty-four and sixty-eight hours. Their kitchen houses were rented at between 3s. 6d. and 4s. 6d. a week, sometimes accommodating two families each. There was no expectation of holidays and even a tram ride was a luxury. The families of the unskilled formed the majority of the city's population and, as the only significant safety net was the workhouse, their dependence on volunteer activity remained very great.[31]

Much volunteer activity in these years was thrown into the campaigns for and against Home Rule and drilling in the Irish Volunteers and the Ulster Volunteer Force. During the Great War all the Irish recruits to the armed forces were volunteers. In the Belfast-Antrim area Catholics were actually more likely to take the king's shilling than their Protestant neighbours. Then, from the summer of 1920 Belfast was convulsed by political and sectarian violence. In Belfast 236 people were killed in the first few months of 1922 alone.

The post-war slump which set in during the winter of 1920-21 became a protracted depression as Northern Ireland began its life as the UK's first devolved region. Around one fifth of insured workers were unemployed throughout the 1920s and during the 1930s at least a quarter were out of work – just under 30 per cent in 1938. The Northern Ireland, teetering on the edge of bankruptcy, found that it could not match the level of social services provided on the other side of the Irish Sea. The insured unemployed got the dole, the 'b'roo', for six months only. Then they had to survive on 'outdoor relief' provided by the Board of Guardians. The result was that the health of the poor actually declined. Maternal mortality actually rose by one-fifth between 1922 and 1938. Infant mortality in Belfast was 96 per 1,000 compared with 59 per 1,000 in Sheffield. The most feared disease, the main killer of young adults, was tuberculosis: Belfast' death rate from this disease was higher than in any UK city and higher even than in Dublin.[32]

Probably the bulk of beneficial voluntary work in these years was provided by the churches. St Vincent de Paul Society was particularly energetic in Catholic districts and it was reckoned that visits by that organisation's volunteers were worth 3s. 6d. a week to a distressed family.[33] From the Grosvenor Hall, the Methodist Church's Belfast Central Mission distributed food – the committee was told that in March 1933 'five tons of potatoes were distributed in one stone lots – none were bought', and in December 1934 around 300 dinners were being given daily to adults and children, either free or at a charge of one penny each.[34]

The Second World War called for a fresh surge of volunteer activity, particularly after more than a thousand citizens lost their lives and around half the city's houses were either destroyed or damaged during the German air raids of 1941. Increasingly, however, the state was stepping in and by the end of the war the inhabitants of Belfast were being better fed than ever before. The introduction of the welfare state thereafter (particularly the replacement of the Poor Law by the Health Service in 1938-39) brought about the most striking improvement in living standards in the century. The official safety net became ever more widely spread but it was never without sizeable holes which needed to be filled by volunteering.

FRIEND OF HAIG POPPY DAY FUND

Mrs Susan Chambers, 27 Hopewell Street, Belfast, whose funeral took place on Saturday to Dundonald, was in her 81st year.

For 27 years she was organiser of Woodvale and Shankhill district for the Lord Haig Poppy Day Appeal Fund.

During the war she collected for the Red Cross and St Dunstan's also the British Sailors' Society.

Mrs Chambers who was a member of Woodvale and Court Ward Unionist Association, also a member of Fernhill Women's L.O.L. 127, is survived by her husband, five daughters and two sons.

Obituary of Mrs Susan Chambers, volunteer for the Lord Haig Poppy Day Appeal Fund and others, Belfast Telegraph 1953

A particular feature of the decades following the Second World War was that a great many organisations which received some public funding still depended very heavily on the unpaid efforts of volunteers, the great majority of them not receiving travel or other out-of-pocket expenses. An example is the Northern Ireland Marriage Guidance Council founded in the Lord Mayor's Parlour on 4 September 1947. Its counselling work started in the offices of the Belfast Council of Social Welfare. Income was £575 9s 7d (raised from subscriptions, donations and sales of work) in 1948 when 103 cases were considered. After much negotiation, the Ministry of Home Affairs gave a grant of £150 in 1950. The proportion of public funding grew and by 1968 half the organisation's income was derived from the Ministry of Home Affairs, Belfast Corporation and Down County Council. The Marriage Guidance Council (which changed its name to Relate Northern Ireland in 1988) did not have a full-time Director until 1976 and depended overwhelmingly on volunteering.[35]

Other publicly-funded bodies which depended heavily on unpaid volunteers included: the Belfast City and District Water Commissioners (the 'Water Office', 1 Donegall Square North); Belfast Harbour Commissioners (Harbour Office); the Northern Ireland Housing Trust (12 Hope Street); the Northern Ireland Tourist Board (Royal Avenue); the Arts Council (1 Joy Street), which included the Lord Mayor on its committee; the Belfast Education Committee; and the Ulster Savings Committee, 'a voluntary body appointed by the Ministry of Finance for Northern Ireland. Its terms of reference include educating and encouraging the people of Northern Ireland in thrift through investment in State Guaranteed Securities, which include Savings Certificates, Ulster Development Bonds, Defence Bonds and deposits in the Savings Banks, etc.'.

Bryson House in Bedford Street emerged as the hub of Belfast's charitable activity and volunteering. The Belfast Council of Social Welfare, operating from Bryson House, had been founded in 1906 and provided 'a bureau of information on all matters relating to social welfare' and co-ordinated the work of 'of the different charitable bodies in

THE COMPANIES ACT (NORTHERN IRELAND), 1932.

BELFAST COUNCIL OF SOCIAL WELFARE
(INCORPORATED).

MEMORANDUM OF ASSOCIATION

1. The name of the Association is " BELFAST COUNCIL OF SOCIAL WELFARE (INCORPORATED)."

2. The Registered Office of the Association will be situate in Northern Ireland.

3. The objects for which the Association is established are:—

(a) To take over and absorb the Charitable Organisation which has existed in the City of Belfast under the name of " Belfast Council of Social Welfare (Incorporating Belfast Charity Organisation Society)," which has used as a short title " Belfast Council of Social Welfare," and to carry on and continue the work and methods of the said Organisation, and to acquire and take over the whole assets and liabilities thereof, or such of them as the Association may legally acquire and take over, and with a view thereto to execute all documents which may be requisite for that purpose..

(b) To form a centre of communication between all Charitable and Benevolent Institutions in the City of Belfast and neighbourhood and all public and local authorities and other agencies and persons interested in Charity and in the poor in the said City and neighbourhood, so as to co-ordinate such charitable effort, both voluntary and official, and to prevent, as far as possible, the overlapping of effort; to direct charitable effort into the most fruitful channels, to educate the public in all matters affecting the social welfare of the poor, and to aid generally in the improvement of the condition of the poor.

(c) To prevent and check vagrancy, begging, and imposture, and if deemed expedient or necessary, to expose the same, and to prosecute or assist in the prosecution of the offenders.

(d) To promote, support or oppose such Bills as may be promoted in the Parliament of Northern Ireland or proposed to be promoted in the said Parliament, Provisional Orders or other measures affecting or calculated to be likely to affect directly or indirectly any of the objects of the Association.

Memorandum and Articles of Association of Belfast Council of Social Welfare, 3 January 1939

Belfast and prevents overlapping'. The Northern Ireland Marriage Guidance Council was based there until it moved to 76 Dublin Road in 1967. Bryson House served as the meeting place for the Federation of Women's Institutes of Northern Ireland; though it described itself as 'an organisation for countrywomen whose aim is to co-operate in promoting any work which makes for the betterment of their homes and the improvement of conditions of rural life', it had a keen urban membership involved in organising cultural talks, discussions and visits in addition to traditional jam, marmalade and cake making. Abbeyfield Belfast Society, operating from Bryson House, provided 'small houses, in their own neighbourhood, for elderly tenants, who are lonely and without relatives who can accommodate them'. Also based in Bryson House, the Extra Care Committee for the Aged and Lonely, founded in 1958, aimed 'to try to alleviate some of the hardship and, particularly, the loneliness of the elderly of Belfast by regular visiting and provision for needs not covered by the statutory bodies'. Other organisations in Bryson House included the Northern Ireland Committee of the Freedom from Hunger Campaign, Wireless for the Bedridden (Belfast Branch), the Youth Hostel Association of Northern Ireland, the Northern Ireland Association of Boys' Clubs, and the Belfast Garden Plots Association for 'the provision of garden plots for working men'.

Sport, particularly for the young, relied on volunteers giving their time during evenings and weekends. The County Antrim Gaelic Athletic Association was particularly active in Belfast; sport and fitness programmes were at the core of the City of Belfast YMCA's numerous

The Belfast Natural History and Philosophical Society Publicity Brochure 2008

activities in Wellington Place; and other sporting organisations based in the city included the Irish Football Association (20 Windsor Avenue), the Irish Boxing Association, the Irish Football League (16 Donegall Square South), the Irish Hockey Union, the Ulster Branch of the Irish Intermediate Football League, the Ulster Council of the Irish Lawn Tennis Association, the Ulster Branch of the Irish Rugby Football Union (58 Howard Street), the Northern Cricket Union of Ireland, and the Knock Motor Cycle and Car Club. The Northern Ireland Branch of the National Playing Fields Association (109 Royal Avenue) had as its stated object 'to urge the need for more playing fields and children's playgrounds...and helps financially within the limits of its resources'.

Other organisations were variously concerned with the preservation of heritage, scientific progress, civic education and moral welfare. The gentry were well represented on the committee of the National Trust (82 Dublin Road) in 1963 but also included the flamboyant editor of the Belfast Telegraph, John E Sayers, C E B Brett (already an authority on Belfast's historic buildings) and the northern officer of the Irish Congress of Trade Unions, Billy Blease (later Lord Blease). The Belfast Civic Society, formed in 1943, set out 'to render such services in the City of Belfast and adjacent districts as are calculated to stimulate civic interest and a sense of responsibility, with a view to a) increasing the amenities of the city and adjacent districts b) preserving buildings and monuments of historic or artistic worth and places of natural beauty'. The Belfast Natural History and Philosophical Society, formed back in 1821 'for the cultivation of that science by means of papers and lectures, and more particularly in the investigation of the Natural History of Ireland', had handed over its museum collection to form the nucleus of the Ulster Museum in Stranmillis. Its President in 1963 was Dr R W M Strain, the distinguished historian of the Belfast Charitable Society.

Volunteers involved themselves in a kaleidoscope of societies ranging from the Alpine Society (Ulster Group) 'to further knowledge about alpine and rock plants', the Belfast Naturalists' Field Club (Old Museum, College Square North), the British Legion (67 Lisburn Road), the British Order of Ancient Gardeners' Friendly Society (Belfast District), the Irish Temperance League (20 Lombard Street), the Rotary Club (Grand Central Hotel, Royal Avenue), the Theosophical Society in Northern Ireland (18 Brookhall Avenue), the Ulster Folklife Society (28 Bedford Street), the Ulster-Scot Historical Society (Law Courts), the Young Women's Christian Association for Ireland (Belfast Branch, 3-5 Malone Road), and the Soroptimist Club of Belfast 'which is for women...to encourage and foster high ethical standards in business and professional life'.

Belfast may not have been, as had been claimed in the previous century, the 'Athens of the North', but it was by no means a cultural desert. In 1968 the Governor of Northern Ireland, Lord Wakehurst, was Patron of several cultural organisations including the Belfast Philharmonic Society (2 Wellington Place). Amateur drama flourished, its principal group of players being the Drama Circle (The Studio, 179a New Lodge Road). Other organisations included: the Grand Opera Society of Northern Ireland, founded in 1957; the Classical Society, founded in 1928 'to further the study of the life and literature of Classical Greece and Rome'; P.E.N. (Belfast), with actor/writers Jack McQuoid and Richard Hayward as leading lights; the Royal Ulster Academy of Arts (7 College Square North); the Belfast Burns Association; and the Poetry Society Northern Ireland Centre which sought 'to interest and bind together lovers of poetry through the English-speaking world'.

The Ulster Arts Club (90 Lisburn Road, had been founded in 1902 to 'further the cause of art by promoting the social intercourse of persons practising or having a sympathetic interest in any of the arts, whether pure or applied'. In 1963 its President was the senior civil servant, Patrick Shea – one of the few Catholics (outside bodies not organised by or closely associated with the Catholic Church) in a prominent volunteering position. Inevitably, in a divided society, volunteer activity was to a great extent channelled through the denominations. An exception was the Samaritans which had as its Deputy Directors Rev. J R Musgrave (Presbyterian), Rev. W S Callaghan (Methodist), and Rev. H P Murphy (Catholic). The Samaritans were 'a voluntary organisation for those tempted to suicide or despair. Any person in great despair may be given friendship and help at any time, day or night'.

One of the biggest Catholic institutions was Nazareth House (352 Ormeau Road) which

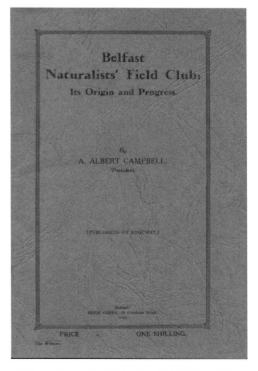

A history of the Belfast Naturalists' Field Club published by A Albert Campbell in 1938.

provided 'a happy and comfortable home for aged poor, also orphan girls'. It accommodated around three hundred in the late 1960s. The Mother Superior permitted visiting every day between 2 p.m. and 5 p.m. 'The House has no funds', she stated, 'and depends entirely for support on voluntary contributions'. Also run by nuns and depending on voluntary contributions was Nazareth Lodge on the Ravenhill Road which was a home for 150 boys from two to eleven years.[36] In the twenty years after the Second World War Belfast retained what was by British standards a very high level of church attendance. This was particularly true of Catholics. A survey conducted among undergraduates of Queen's University in 1959 showed that church attendance figures were 94 per cent for Catholics compared with 64 per cent for Methodists, 59 per cent for Presbyterians and 46 per cent for members of the Church of Ireland. Did these figures reflect attendance for the population as a whole? It seems that attendance at Protestant churches was lower than these figures suggest – in 1908 only one in fifteen in Ballymacarrett were thought to attend church.[37] It does seem that in Belfast attendance at church by Catholics in the 1960s was over 90 per cent and it is clear that most volunteering by Catholics was done through church organisations.

The Protestant Orphan Society for the Counties of Antrim and Down (10 May Street) was only one of an extraordinary range of denominational organisations. Several 'missions' were concerned not only to propagate the Gospel but also to provide for the poor and the lonely of all religions, including: Belfast Central Mission, Grosvenor Hall; Missions to Seamen (81 Corporation Street); North Belfast Mission (37 Great George's Street), with a 'People's Hall' in York Street – 'an all-the-year round relief service is carried on here' it declared; and the Shankill Road Mission (114-116 Shankill Road) which stated that 'every year hundreds of needy

families are visited and helped, and food parcels at Christmas are distributed to homes of the poor'.

Youth organisations, too, tended to be denominational. The Down and Connor Catholic Youth Council (28 Cyprus Avenue) had Father P. McCann as its Secretary. The Catholic Boy Scouts and Girl Guides had their Protestant counterparts (headquarters 50 Dublin Road), the Boys' Brigade and Lifeboys (14 May Street), and the Girls' Brigade (9 Upper Queen Street). Other Protestant youth organisations included the Churches' Youth Welfare Society and the Church Lads' Brigade. Rises in the school leaving age from 1947 actually kept young people apart from 'the other sort' for longer than before. Then in 1969 the tensions in this deeply divided city gushed violently to the surface and, as Northern Ireland became the most continuously disturbed region of western Europe since 1945, the demand for beneficial volunteering became especially urgent.

Boys warming their hands. Photo: Stanley Matchett

Endnotes

1 Jonathan Bardon, A History of Ulster, Belfast (1992) pp. 35-36, 47; Raymond Gillespie, Early Belfast: The origins and growth of an Ulster town to 1750, Belfast (2007), pp 53-123

2 R.M. Young (ed), The Town Book of Belfast, Belfast (republished 2009)

3 Jonathan Bardon, A History of Ireland in 250 Episodes, Dublin (2008), pp. 248-251

4 Jean Agnew, Belfast Merchant Families in the Seventeenth Century, Dublin (1996), p. 67

5 Ibid., pp. 57 and 230

6 R.W.M. Strain, Belfast and its Charitable Society: A Story of Urban Social Development, Oxford, 1961, pp. 19-21

7 Ibid., pp. 29-96; Jonathan Bardon, An Interesting and Honourable History: The Belfast Charitable Society: The First 250 Years, 1752-2002, Belfast (2002), pp. 11-19

8 Jonathan Bardon, op. cit. (1992), pp. 216-236

9 Mary McNeill, The Life and Times of Mary Ann McCracken 1770-1866, Dublin (1960), pp. 257-287

10 Public Record Office of Northern Ireland, Problems of a Growing City: Belfast 1780-1870, Belfast (1973), p. xii

11 Jonathan Bardon, Belfast: an illustrated history, Belfast (1982), pp. 66-155

12 PRONI, op. cit., p. xiii

13 Strain, op. cit., pp. 182-211; Bardon, op. cit., (2002), pp. 26-29

14 PRONI, op. cit., p. 224

15 Ibid., p. 235

16 Ibid., pp. 235-7

17 Alison Jordan, Who Cared? Charity in Victorian & Edwardian Belfast, Belfast (1987), pp. 25-26

18 Ibid., p. 27

19 Bardon, op. cit. (1982), p. 98

20 Ibid., p. 99

21 PRONI, op. cit., pp. 242-243

22 Jordan op. cit., pp. 29-30

23 Bardon (1982) op. cit., p. 92

24 Jordan op. cit., pp. 37-38

25 Ibid., p. 40

26 Ibid., pp. 41-48

27 Ibid., pp. 97-98

28 Ibid., p. 106

29 Jonathan Bardon, Belfast: A Century, Belfast (1999), pp. viii, 1-3; Jonathan Bardon in Frederick W. Boal and Stephen A. Royle (eds), Enduring City: Belfast in the Twentieth Century, Belfast (2006), pp. 275-276

30 Belfast and Ulster Directory, 1901, 1903, 1907

31 Bardon in Boal and Royle (eds.) op. cit., p. 276

32 Munck, Ronnie, and Bill Rolston, Belfast in the Thirties: An Oral History, Belfast (1987) pp. 60, 70-75

33 A.C. Hepburn, A Past Apart: Studies in the History of Catholic Belfast 1850-1950, Belfast (1996), p. 14

34 Eric Gallagher, At Points of Need: the story of the Belfast Central Mission 1889-1989, Belfast (1989), p. 69

35 Relate Northern Ireland – Historical Notes, Relate NI files, 1998; Northern Ireland Marriage Guidance Council Annual Report 1968

36 Belfast and Ulster Directory, 1963

37 W A Maguire, Belfast, Belfast (1993), p. 176; Jonathan Bardon in Boal and Royle op. cit., p. 276

VSB TIMELINE

In 1966 Denis Barritt who was Secretary of the Belfast Council of Social Welfare (Bryson House) visited Manchester and Salford Council of Social Service Volunteer Bureau. On his return BCSW Executive Committee discussed how to set up a similar Volunteer Bureau (VSB) and it was not long before they put in place a system to recruit, train and place volunteers. In 1967 the Clement Wilson Foundation gave a grant which enabled the appointment of Mrs Pru Peskett as a part-time organiser. This timeline highlights the key developments of VSB.

The 80s

- In response to high unemployment (in 1982 the unemployment rate was over 21%), VSB developed a Youth Opportunities Programme and an Action for Community Employment (ACE) Scheme. Both provided valuable work experience and skills training. The YOP moved to become an independent organisation and in 2009 operates as Youth Training Workshop in Donegall Street.

- The ACE Scheme operated for over 10 years and employed 1500-2000 individuals on one-year contracts. Their work was of a practical nature and of immense value – particularly for older people. In 1986 ACE Care Attendants visited 70 homes on a weekly basis, 2141 rooms were decorated and 7,690 visits were made to maintain gardens.

- Introduce the Home Security Scheme, a service provided by volunteers

The 60s

- With a grant from a Charitable Foundation of £750 VSB is started in April 1967 with a part-time Co-ordinator and nine volunteers.

- By April 1968, 217 volunteers have been recruited, with 2/3 being under 21.

- Books-on-Wheels introduced for house-bound in conjunction with the Central Library – 40 Volunteer Drivers recruited for the service.

- Furniture Service - supplied items of second hand furniture to those most in need and a removal service often offered the only lifeline to families facing intimidation. In 1974, two vans were on the road driven by volunteers and travelling in excess of 3,000 miles a month.

- Developed a Long Term Volunteer Programme (LTV) offering young adults voluntary placements of six months to one year

- " In the late 1960s the development of the Voluntary Service Bureau brought a new type of volunteer to Bryson House - young people in jeans! Apparently some of the old volunteers and employees complained about the behaviour of the young and tact had to be exercised."

Ref: Vision and Venture - A History of Bryson House Charitable Grant by Catherine Charley.

The 70s

- VSB introduce to Belfast local community Summer Play Schemes – staffed by local volunteers and young people from various parts of the world. In 1970, 80 volunteers from 19 different countries took part.

- Over the next decade more than 1,000 volunteers were involved in delivering a host of creative summer activities to 15,000 children.

- The Summer Playschemes introduced the first Bouncy Castle inflatable to Northern Ireland.

- Playbuses introduced to Northern Ireland by VSB – a Double Decker bus converted to act as a Mobile Nursery. By 1974 there were four on the road. Playbuses were supposed to be a temporary solution for the lack of childcare facilities – they eventually came off the road some 30 years later.

- Women Caring Trust established and VSB played a role in supporting the Trust to administer its small grants programme in Northern Ireland. They have raised and distributed over £2 million.

- Developed a Volunteer Befriending Scheme and Transport Service.

- VSB move to new premises on the Lisburn Road.

The 90s

- Retired and Senior Volunteer Programme established.
- Young Citizens in Action established and a very successful 'Use your Head, Use your Vote' campaign.
- WheelWorks Youth Arts Project created and the Mobile Art Cart purchased.
- The Ian Gow Memorial Fund was established and VSB provided the administrative base and support to the local NI Committee. During its 10 years over 2,000 grants were given to individual young people to assist them with education, volunteering, or to help overcome a particular crisis or hardship.
- Launched Good Practice Guidelines for Volunteer Befriending Schemes.

The 2000s

- Moved to new modern building in Shaftesbury Square to increase profile of volunteering and to recruit more individuals.
- Developed Employer Supported Volunteering and to date 2,500 individuals have been involved.
- Took responsibility for the delivery of the Volunteer Centres for North Down and Ards and Fermanagh
- Successfully incorporated People First – a volunteer driving organisation in North Down. Each year volunteers undertake 4000 journeys and travel 100,000 miles
- Five volunteers operated a charity shop on the Andersonstown Road 2000-2006 generating £150,000.
- Developed a partnership with the North & West Belfast Health & Social Services Trust – a capacity building programme for older people.
- Gained Investing In Volunteers accreditation.
- Developed a Volunteer Transport Buddy Scheme
- Celebrated 40 Years to recognise the 50,000 people who passed through VSB on their personal volunteer journey.

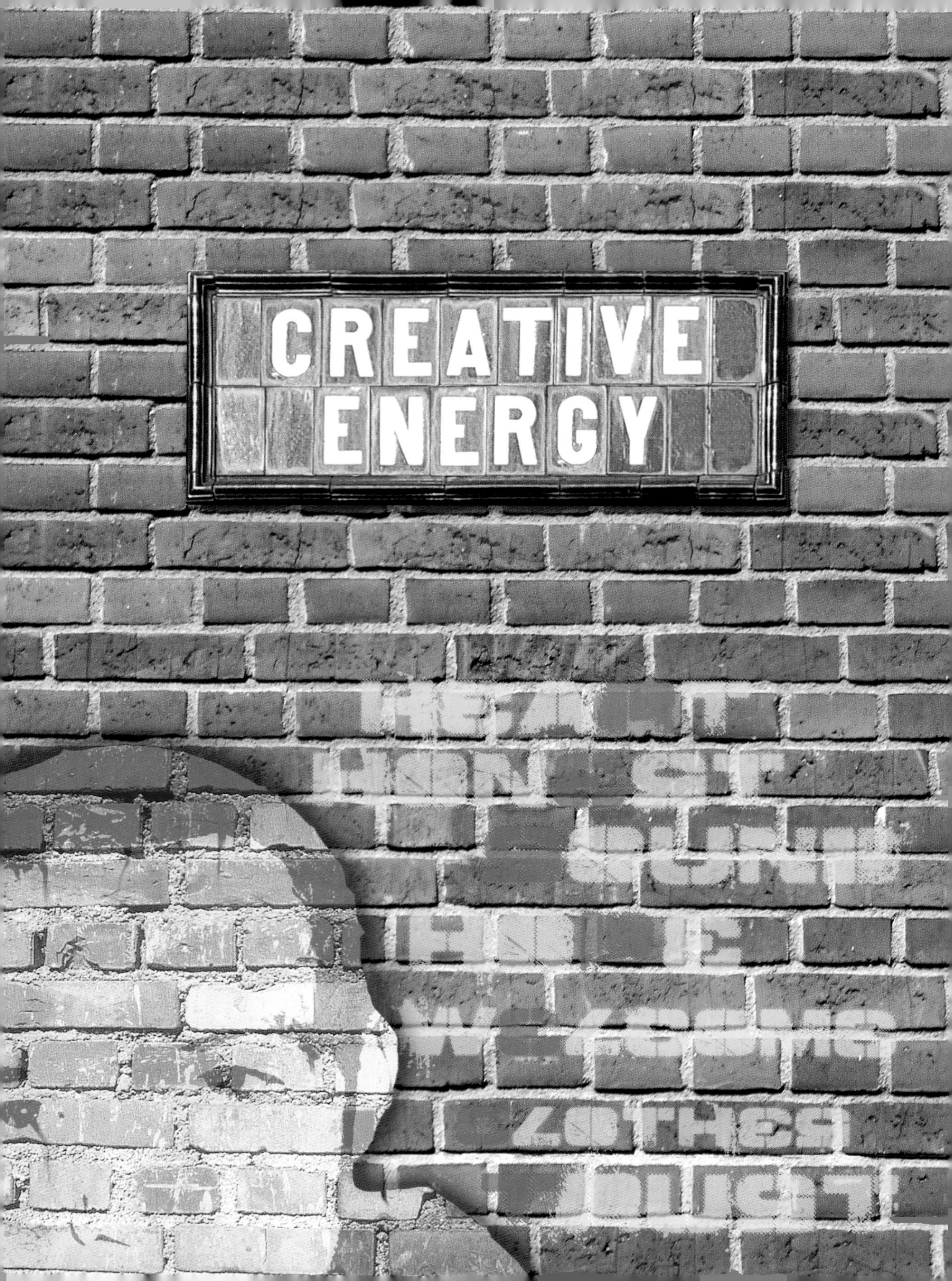
CREATIVE
ENERGY

AT ONE TIME
A personal reflection by Gerald Dawe

The two who called to our front door are probably well into their late fifties and early sixties by now. My mother was expecting the call but when the door bell rang we were both still taken a little by surprise. Could she allow me to join a band? I would be well looked after. I would need a black polo neck and dark trousers. There'd be rehearsals after Scouts, and occasional weekends. She agreed and thus began my very brief career as a singer in a 'rock' band. It probably didn't last more that six months and I played I think about three times on stage 'live', so to speak. Two or three cover songs of 'Gloria' (what else?), The Kinks 'All day and all of the night', 'Let's spend the Night together' by The Rolling Stones. The rest of the set were instrumentals – 'Apache' and 'Wipe Out' which showed how good our drummer was. The band, The Trolls, was a four piece outfit – bass player (Geordie), lead guitarist (Eric), drummer (Roger) and singer (yours truly). There may have been a further fifth member but that's how I recall it, forty years on. Our practice sessions took place in a house on the Cave Hill Road and in the Scout hall of the 78th Duncairn

troop, down a laneway that ran parallel to Glandore Avenue and in behind a row of shops (at one time), including a Jewish hairdresser and delicatessen on the Antrim road.

The only 'real' memory I have of actually singing was in a talent competition in a hotel on the main street in Bangor. To liven things up I had maracas which I shook while moving about on stage. The previous night a show band (The Royal, I think) had inadvertently split one of the timbers on stage in which my prancing foot had momentarily stuck, taking a little of the polish off my performance, if one can call it that. Most things were made up as we went along, except for the order of songs (of which there was only a very limited number); what happened in between and during was unrehearsed; moveable. Anyway we came in second on the 'Applause Meter'; a simple device which was manually worked according to the volume of applause the judge interpreted as greeting on stage each of the representatives from the various performers and 'acts'. I was the mascot that night in Bangor and I can still remember my sense of disbelief as I watched the judge work a pedal as the applause meter flashed into action like a fairground gadget and then fell back to zero as he took his inspired foot off the pedal! 'Second' wasn't so bad after all; indeed things could have been worse.

In the van back to Belfast we inadvertently parked for a pit stop on the crest of a hill and luckily no one stepped out of the back as the unprotected siding gave on to a severe drop of a couple of hundred foot down an embankment. That would have been a more serious dint to our pride.

Through the band I met a few other lads, slightly older than my fifteen years in 1967, many of whom were, like me, in the scouts. The 'troop' was culturally mixed, and friends I made there came from Protestant and Jewish backgrounds in the lower- and middle-class neighbourhoods of north Belfast. My own family had lived in the area since the turn of the last century and had, in the form of my mother's great grandparents prospered, living in a substantial home at the top of Duncairn Gardens (since demolished) and my grandmother (with whom my mother, sister and I lived) having returned from Canada and London and finally settled with her widowed mother, in Skegoneill, literally around the corner from the Scout's Hall off the Antrim Road.

This was 'my' part of Belfast, from the mid-fifties to the late sixties. Through the landscape, streets, histories, customs and lifestyle of that culturally mixed and varied class mini-society, I discovered myself and ultimately the complex meaning of northern Irish society. But back to The Trolls.

I think it was through the band that I joined, as a fifteen year old, the PPU (Peace Pledge Union), took in the last hoorah of the CND (Campaign for Nuclear Disarmament), first came in contact with NICPV (the Northern Ireland Campaign for Peace in Vietnam), attended occasional 'fast' sessions outside the City Hall, handing out leaflets and on

Flower People, Botanic Gardens, Belfast. Photo: Stanley Matchett

Sunday nights, sat in Heaven, the white church at the side of the City Hall, drinking tea and chatting up girls.

Central to much of this campaigning was Orangefield Boys School, in east Belfast, where daily I bussed across from my north-side home, along with significant numbers of other students from all over Belfast: Stranmillis, Ballygomartin, Malone, as well as its immediate hinterland of Castlereagh, Beersbridge, Newtownards and Braniel roads. The school had a reputation for liberal and progressive educational policies and was noted for the quality of teaching staff, working under the visionary headmaster, John Malone – 'Dai' Francis, Davey Hammond, the Sinnerton brothers, Jonathan Bardon and Sam McCready who set in motion the Lyric Youth theatre which produced out of Orangefield a generation of talented actors and others involved in the radio, television, theatre and film world (including my old friend, Gary Williamson, who worked alongside Denis Potter for many years as set designer).

The other important figure in those mid-sixties days was Terri Hooley, whom I had briefly met in a small, very small office, at the top of a rickety stairway in a building in High Street. The Ba'ai faith was in an office below him. From here Terri sent out his willing troops to advise the good people of Belfast about the inequities of Vietnam.

We even had a Vietnamese flag on display

> *I discovered myself and ultimately the complex meaning of northern Irish society.*

although on one occasion I recall when a counter-demonstration took place outside the City Hall involving some protestant fundamentalists, they took exception to the flag, and one of their number lifted it from its holder, denouncing us as communists and the devil knows what. He had not however reckoned on the swift and physical retaliation of a somewhat inebriated sailor who had temporarily taken us under his wing, applauding whatever he could make out from the mashed exhortations being shouted down our loud speaker. A nifty head-butt sprawled the thin-faced, previously ecstatic, now ashen faced, preacher, and our flag was promptly restored to its rightful place. Our proselytizing competitor slipped further along the City Hall railings to where the flower-sellers were packing up for the day.

Saturday late afternoons were like that. Across the road a young man selling 'Free Citizen' somewhat later in, maybe '68, was goaded and prodded and finally smacked by three or four men who were far from happy with his shouts of complaint against the northern state. I can still hear his brave young voice, frightened yet unbowed, at the corner of Gilpin's in Royal Avenue, and the women who surrounded him, and patted him and helped him back to his feet.

Out of these disparate little groups of sixties hopes and fears, experiments and fascinations, on the periphery of which I observed with keen interest, the social life of Belfast changed and from the viewpoint of the young, tuned in to the big world of British and, particularly, American popular culture and politics. My own interest in politics ebbed and flowed and because of this vacillation I never really stuck at any one thing for any length of time. The popular culture

Ulster's Top Ten

1. — BABY COME BACK — The Equals.
2. — SON OF HICKORY HOLLER'S TRAMP — O. C. Smith.
3. — I PRETEND — Des. O'Connor.
4. — YUMMY YUMMY YUMMY — Ohio Express.
5. — YESTERDAY HAS GONE — Cupid's Inspirations.
6. — MY NAME IS JACK — Manfred Mann.
7. — HURDY-GURDY MAN — Donovan.
8. — BLUE EYES — Don Partridge.
9. — WHY BOBBY KENNEDY WHY — Hilton Showband.
10. — JUMPING JACK FLASH — Rolling Stones.

Cityweek, July 1968

was defining and probably at its peak on both radio and television as well as producing some of the best in 'pop' music. When The Trolls disappeared, and the scouts, folk music came into the frame with real life sessions scattered around the city centre in pubs and clubs and a couple of private homes, but this was towards the end of the sixties, just before the curtain fell and the Troubles took over all our lives.

There was a brief period of immense freedom when Belfast, including the north of the city, in which young men and women from all kinds of religious backgrounds (and none) mixed – at parties when parents were away, after school in coffee bars in town, outside shops on the Antrim road, crisscrossing town for a date, going to the 'flicks', and of course, the endless listening to music and of dancing, forever dancing.

For the music scene in Belfast was *the scene*. Whatever happened in the front rooms, drawing rooms, back bedrooms, attics, of the houses were all these young men and women, dressed in the various fashions of the time, reading the same rock magazines, buying the same albums, the idea that in five or six years their lives would be ruled by sectarian overlords, paramilitary courts, or that political passions would led some of their number to maim and murder fellow citizens, was simply beyond belief. It still catches me out, I have to say. The vortex of the Troubles which was building up under the surface of Belfast life of that time was built on powerful resentments and generations of injustice and mistrust. We were like tight rope walkers who kept looking forward, we never looked back. If the world was at fault it was Vietnam, the Bomb, but what this wee city of Belfast was, was home, girls, music, clothes, Bangor, Portrush, the sea, the sand. The pubs: Kelly's Cellars, The Olde

House, The Scrumpy Rooms, The Fiddler's. Sitting upstairs in the Queen's Arcade pub and looking down on a Saturday afternoon as shoppers milled about and a war veteran mouthed into his harmonica looking for a few pennies. Sammy Houston's; The Maritime; Inst; the Floral Hall. Dances; dancing galore. And Top of the Pops, Ready, Steady, Go; 6.5 Special; Play for Today. And all those great bands playing the Ulster Hall. You name it. They all played here. Not unionism or nationalism. Not history. Not 1690. Not 1916. What was all that about? It was not willful blindness so much as youthful ignorance and maybe an instinctive desire not to be cowed by the past.

Calling in with a friend to a house at the junction of Antrim Road and Duncairn Gardens to meet up with our girls of the time, we were invited in to the fine house of comfortable welcoming proportions. As we stood momentarily in the hallway of that typical Belfast Victorian home, a large painting of Our Lord, with votive lamp underneath it, glowed in the dusk of early evening, and rhythmic sounds came out from the pantry. We exchanged perplexed glances, hunched shoulders and in a moment our girls appeared, radiant in their mini skirts and blouses and dancing shoes after reciting the rosary, and we made the bus, heading straight for town and Betty Staffs or the Jazz Club.

On Saturday nights I would call for my friend Lou and wait for his evening supper and prayers to be complete before we'd head off; once or twice joining in with yarmulke on, not having the faintest clue what was happening. We might collect on the way Ken, whose father had fought as a rear-gunner in the big aerial battles of WW2 and walk passed the imposing Church at the corner of Skegoneill and Antrim Road towards Somerton or Downview or back through Glandore, passed so many different homes, to meet up with someone else - Protestants and Catholics and Jews; lapsed this and that. Gospel halls, Saved by the Blood of the Lamb. A synagogue. A British legion hall. A Catholic convent girls' school. A Protestant secondary school. It just went on and on. Grammar school, corner shop, lounge bar, hotel, gardens, entries, until we hopped another bus and were in town by 7.30pm.

And all over the city the same thing was happening. Young men and women in their teens and early twenties were thinking about Saturday night, not Monday morning, or Sunday service. That vibrant life spread throughout that generation in 1967 and maybe there was an awareness that something new was breaking through and that we didn't need to worry or complain about 'where' you were 'from', what school you went to, in order to sort and file under Protestant, Catholic, Jew, dissenter, unionist, nationalist, orange, green… I don't think it mattered then, not to us. Later, unquestionably; but not then, no. We had a ball, no matter what anyone says. The chance was briefly in the air. As we know, at the close of the sixties, Belfast fell into a time-warp; forty years later, it looks like it just might, with a bit of luck, be back on track again.

The Belfast Music Tour 2009 poster

present

STRIKE HAPPY

A FARCICAL COMEDY BY DUNCAN GREENWOOD

— IN —

THE BELVOIR PARISH HALL

— ON —

MONDAY, TUESDAY & WEDNESDAY

15th, 16th & 17th October, 1973

Nightly at 8 p.m.

★ *HILARIOUS DOMESTIC COMEDY*

★ *2 HOURS NON STOP LAUGHTER*

★ *YOU CAN'T AFFORD TO MISS THIS ONE*

Subscription   -   All Seats 20p

RICHARD MILLS *Belvoir Players*

I was sitting in the Church Hall at Belvoir – the estate had been built since 1962 and people from all areas, places and backgrounds used the church hall – it was the centre of the community.

I was always interested in performing, and noticed that in the building there was a beautiful stage with red velvet curtains and wondered why there was no amateur theatre company here? That's where this all started – and there's been many turns on the road from then to here.

The first thing we did was three one act plays, to raise some money. All we had was the stage, curtain and chairs, there was no lighting. In 1969 we raised the princely sum of £40.

We worked hard and equipped the hall with a dozen lights and sound system. We used the skills of our members – especially for lighting and sound. Our volunteers bring a wide range of skills that we can tap into.

In 1984 we moved to a barn in Drumbo, a big hayloft. It wasn't that we fell out with the church – I used to joke that we were excommunicated – it was just that sharing a hall was not the best idea. In the hall things can go wrong, we needed somewhere we could be secure.

We met there for 11 years – then in 1995 we realised we had gone as far as we could go with what we had. There was a need for a purpose built

Wedding Fever *by Sam Cree.*
The Group Theatre, Bedford Street closed on Saturday 3 May 2005 with Belvoir Players performance of Wedding Fever by Sam Cree.

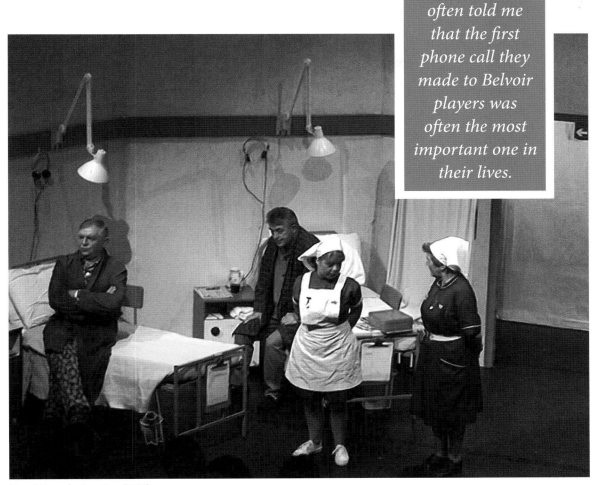

Stop it Nurse *by Sam Cree (2003)*

> *People have often told me that the first phone call they made to Belvoir players was often the most important one in their lives.*

site to rehearse and do performances. We had a vibrant youth group and would organise a car pool. Volunteers used their own motors over and back from the Park Centre to Drumbo.

In 1995 we started working with the youth group out of the council activity centre but it was £5 to £7 each hour, so then we set about getting funding to go to Lottery. A lot of groups were getting up to £5k for equipment from the lottery fund. We decided to go for the jackpot – a centre of excellence for amateur theatre, a HQ for amateur theatre in NI.

We opened the Belvoir Studio in 2000 – and since that have spent another 100k. A variety of people are using it – all sorts of people from all types of organisations. It's been what I would consider one of the best lottery funded facilities in Northern Ireland – in terms of value pound for pound at £475,000.

People have often told me that the first phone call they made to Belvoir players was often the most important one in their lives.

I used to feel like the big daddy – now I feel like the big grand daddy. We have a third generation of volunteers now. People who were children doing panto 30 years ago now have their own children doing panto.

That's the worthwhile bit – not just ticking boxes and filling in forms.

PETER RANKIN *Ulster Architectural Heritage Society*

I have always been interested in houses. As a schoolboy I would draw scale plans of houses, mainly the neo-Georgian. I would go to the Linen Hall Library to look at its collection of books of houses from about 1900 to the First World War. I would borrow these and study them, and then draw scale plans myself. My father used to ask 'Are you sure you don't want to be an architect?' But I said 'No, it's houses like these that interest me, not the sort of architecture I would be likely to be involved with'.

I went to Trinity in Dublin from 1961 to '65 and studied law. I joined the Irish Georgian Society in about 1961 or '62. A few of us formed an Antiques Society at Trinity and held an annual exhibition. With friends I went round the Dublin auctions, and some of those in country houses that we could get to.

In 1965 I came back to Belfast as an apprentice solicitor. Often, when I was at school, and later when I was back living in Belfast I would go out on my bicycle on a Sunday morning before breakfast to take photographs of old buildings in the city and in the country near where I lived.

In late 1966 or early 1967 the idea of forming a 'Victorian Society' in Belfast was being contemplated. The original idea had been Alistair Rowan's (he hasn't received much credit subsequently for it), but as Alistair did not then live in Northern Ireland it was Charles Brett who with Lady Dunleath and others took the idea forward. Charlie asked me to go onto a steering group or committee. In the event the steering group decided to call the society the 'Ulster Architectural Heritage Society' so as to not tie itself to any one particular period of architecture or interest.

Above: Dr A Rowan, Mr P J Rankin, Lady Dunleath and Mr Philip Bell study the Ulster Architectural Heritage society report which they compiled.

The inaugural meeting took place at the Belfast Harbour Office on 17th November 1967, and at that meeting I was elected on to the society's first committee.

One of our priorities was to conserve what there was of good architecture. Around the autumn of 1967 Charles Brett published his 'Buildings of Belfast 1700-1914' to record and raise awareness of what Belfast had in terms of architectural interest and merit: until then Belfast people had had an inferiority complex about its architecture, and thought it had nothing of merit – it was thought correct to despise, to make fun of the City Hall as a bit of imperial neo-baroque bombast: it is in fact a pretty good and well-scaled building.

We had regular committee meetings, and worked at trying to get people actively concerned and involved – the meetings were always fun as well as getting through serious business, so attendance rates were high. We held activities for members –

and after quite a few years we got our membership up to about 1,000. The society now has around 1500 members and continues to run a regular programme of events. I was involved for many years, holding the position of Honorary Treasurer and then Honorary Secretary.

One of the first things the UAHS achieved was the listing of buildings for the Queen's University area of Belfast. By 1968 to '69 we were having some influence on how Queen's regarded its properties. And we would get asked to council meetings to advise places like Craigavon, Antrim and Ballymena on the heritage of buildings in their designated areas and what should be done to preserve them.

Our chairman was the well-known solicitor Charles Brett; we had architects and influential people on the committee like Lady Dunleath; Desmond Hodges, an architect who went on to be in charge of the Georgian buildings in the New Town in Edinburgh; Robert McKinstry, who restored the Grand Opera House; Shane Belford the first chief executive officer of the Tourist Office, who was responsible for the society's original logo and typeface, and the design of its first publications; Professor Potter, Professor of Architecture at Queen's; Paddy Falloon of the Northern Brick Company and Dunadry Inn; Margaret Garner, an amateur historian and writer. From west of the Bann we had people like Joe Tracey, a Derry based architect and Ken Adams from Dungannon. A little later we had Dick Oram, a conservation architect who came from England to work at the new town of Craigavon, and later worked with Historic Buildings for Environment and Heritage Service.

We did take on the planners – not just to fight with them, but to work with them to persuade them of what should be done. Occasionally the battle was lost.

Our legacy is that there are a lot more buildings standing today that would have been lost. Planning often had to take second place to roads. People are not architects, but they began to take notice. We have become more aware of what we have inherited and wish to retain as much as possible of what is good that has survived until now.

One of the real achievements of the Ulster Architectural Heritage Society has been in public awareness. Many more people are now to some extent aware of heritage and environmental matters.

However the number of buildings that still have a future before them has greatly increased. Lots of old buildings have been given a new life, and have been life enhancing as well as providing new facilities. Another good thing is that it has involved a lot of people, and there are several young people on the committees or actively working for the built heritage. People have more interest in visual things, and come to the lectures. They realise they have a role to play in protecting our heritage and buildings.

2007 was our 40th anniversary. To mark it we were very fortunate to get the Belfast Harbour Commissioners once again to allow us to use their building for our celebration – which we did on 17th November 2007, right on the day of our first meeting forty years before. The special guest was Joanna Lumley.

With bodies like the National Trust and the Irish Georgian Society, based in Dublin, the UAHS has overlapping memberships and shared interest.

I'm also involved with the Northern Ireland Branch of the National Art Collections Fund, now known as the Art Fund – a body whose principal purpose is to help raise funds for works of art so that they can be retained in the United Kingdom and seen by the public: the Fund has assisted in the acquisition by art galleries museums and public bodies of many hundreds of paintings and works of art.

> *Our legacy is that there are a lot more buildings standing today that would have been lost.*

MIKE MOLONEY *Belfast Community Circus*

'My mother was a fat women in the circus – 22 stone, with tattoos on 90 per cent of her body; my father was a PORG – a person of restricted growth; my uncle was a sword swallower; my sister was 'half man, half woman' – (very hairy). I lived in 27 different houses before I left for university.

My great grandmother was from Sligo and was asked by a church group to go to Australia and work in a big house. She went, got the Southampton boat and fell foul, literally and figuratively, to a British seaman. When she arrived in Sydney in 1903, pregnant – the church group didn't want a pregnant girl so she was sent to the workhouse in Sydney. There she gave birth to Alfred Anderson.

That child was my grandfather. He was adopted by a family from County Clare who adopted 17 children and gave them a brilliant life along with the name Moloney.

I came to Northern Ireland in 1981. I could juggle and spent three months street performing. It was a travelling life – I was a bit like a gypsy. In circus life, you just want to get fed and a bed for the night.

When I arrived in Belfast in May 1981 the first folk festival was taking place. Bobby Sands was on hunger strike. I'd met up with some teachers and stayed with them for ten days. I had a small 'p' political interest in what was happening. I thought Belfast was not a city – but a collection of little ghettos all stuck together.

I'd fallen in with a good group of people and went to VSB. They were looking for volunteers for their summer scheme. I told them I had an arts degree and teaching degree. They said, 'What do you want to do – work on the Protestant or the Catholic side?' The Protestant side was in need of more men – but they said, 'You've got a Catholic name'. I ended up in Glencairn for eight weeks. It was the summer of Charles and Di's wedding so there were street parties going on. It was a hard working class area – still is.

I was interested in working with young people. I was later based in Short Strand – at the MacArt Centre. Drama was an escape for the children.

About three weeks in, this big bloke came in and said he was looking for the drama group. I introduced myself as Mike, he said 'I'm Donal McKendry.' He was from the Arts Council and had come to do some community arts with the older ones. I watched him and liked what was happening.

Afterwards we went to the pub for a beer and got talking – about how we were just not getting the young guys into drama. I told him about Ray Bolton and the Circus in a Suitcase book. We thought 'let's go down that line'.

The community circus started from that day – not just in community centres, but anywhere and everywhere. There was a movement – a growing awareness of community stuff around the early eighties.

We developed a course in personal development through circus. Young people didn't want to just adopt the values or ideas of their parents – they wanted to rebel, and this was reflected in drama, music and dance in the early eighties.

Hunger Strike funeral. Photo: Stanley Matchett

Circus was the language and it didn't matter what foot you kicked with. There was trapeze, unicycles, stilts. On a Saturday morning you could have 20 kids on unicycles – holding hands – getting across the room. It was all done voluntarily – no one was paid. The dynamic was brilliant. People were crawling out of the woodwork to be a part of it.

At first we made most of the equipment – it was easy enough to make stilts. Then we needed more specialist equipment. We realised that we would need to formalise things. Volunteers can blow in and blow out, but now we needed to get insurance, to get a constitution and a management committee. From an easy going circle of friends, we got a group of tough people interested and intent on making it happen.

There were people like Martin Lynch, the playwright – he was artist in residence at the Lyric at the time, and Sam McCready, at Stranmillis College and Sydney Stewart and Play Resource Warehouse all organizing things. There were people from all areas – from Belfast to Derry – keeping it moving, working all the time, teaching, making it happen.

In 1985 we formally set up the circus with a management committee – that's the year in our records, although it had been developing from 1983. It was a voluntary group for the next eight years until we got the money together for an artistic director.

At that time we were based at the Ormeau Park Recreation Centre just off the Ravenhill Road. The present Youth Circus Director is Paul Quate. He started going there when he was just eleven. His career choice was between the shipyard or juggling – wisely he choose juggling, he's done his share of voluntary work and knows the craic of it and the value.

> *He said 'can you guys come out and set up a circus school in Sarajevo?' They had originally called Cirque de Soleil, and they said 'No, the best place to go is Belfast...'*

The circus growth was all through word of mouth – from parents who were concerned about the kids who don't want to do team sports to healthy outreach programmes across the interfaces.

In 1995 – at the end of the war in Sarajevo – a representative from the Belgian Government rang me. He said 'can you guys come out and set up a circus school in Sarajevo?' They had originally called Cirque de Soleil, and they said 'No, the best place to go is Belfast where they do frontier circus'. Donal, myself and Paula McGrogan who was very involved went out and set up the Sarajevo Circus school. That was an amazing experience.

Through volunteering I learned to understand this country and its people. And it was all good fun.

ROY SNOWDEN *The Nomadic*

The Nomadic (left), Titanic's 'Little Sister'. The last of the once mighty White Star Line

The Nomadic Charitable Trust, Appeal Leaflet 2009

'Personally, I was forced to retire from my work, and the voluntary role of project manager gave me a new interest. It's awful to think that the last remaining link with the Titanic should even be thought of going to the scrapheap. Loads of people came just to witness the ship coming back to Belfast, back to her home where she was built. It was an amazing experience.

Anyone who volunteers on the Nomadic – the ship that served the Titanic – will find that the hairs on the back of their neck will be raised. They leave with the experience that they helped restore the Nomadic; the last ship in the White Star fleet, the only ship still sailing that serviced Titanic.

I'm on the Board of the Nomadic Charitable Trust, which was set up by the Department of Social Development to oversee restoration of the ship. The Nomadic was a tender built to service the large liners sailing from the Port of Cherbourg in France.

It was launched on 20th November 1911 and set sail from Belfast on the same day as the Titanic. She lay idle for some time, until 1972 when she was bought for the sole purpose of being a floating restaurant on the River Seine in Paris. She stayed in that role until 1999 when the owner declared himself bankrupt.

It lay idle for some time, again, and was eventually towed up to Le Havre in 2002, where it stayed until it was bought in January 2006 by auction in Paris. The DSD was the new owner. I was asked would I like to join the society called the Nomadic Preservation Society. I took up the role of project manager. The challenge was to save the Nomadic. We wanted the public at large to be interested in the ship. When we put out word worldwide that we needed volunteers to help restore it we were inundated. We set the task of getting it open for Easter 2007 which was achieved. '

KEVIN McCAVANAGH *St. Agnes' Choral Society*

' I was always interested in musical theatre. I was in the Glens Choral Society for many years, and performed in a lot of Gilbert & Sullivan operas – with a few principal roles.

My daughter was a member of St Agnes' Society. She said they were looking for a new treasurer, and asked would I like to do it – I'm a retired accountant. I said I wouldn't mind working with the existing treasurer for a year – she took that to the next meeting, came back and said 'you're the new treasurer dad'.

That was 1997 – they were putting on the Music Man that year. I was in charge of the finances and working backstage, doing my bit, taking props on and off stage. Although I was the Treasurer, I still had the urge to get on that stage, especially at the Opera House.

In 2001 we put on the Merry Widow. The London director said 'it's time you got on stage'. I was delighted and passed myself off reasonably well. We had a standing ovation – it was very successful.

Since then we've done Carousel, The King and I, Oliver, GiGi, the Gondoliers, Mikado and Anything Goes... singing and dancing on stage – me, a man of 72!

St Agnes Choral Society was formed in 1957 in St Agnes's Parish in West Belfast by Fr Jimmy Black, the parish priest. He wanted to give people a cultural outlet, and since then we have performed shows every year, this is our 51st year.

> *I was in charge of the finances and working backstage, doing my bit, taking props on and off stage. Although I was the Treasurer, I still had the urge to get on that stage, especially at the Opera House.*

We have fifty members – of all creeds, backgrounds and from all over Belfast. St Agnes' provides an outlet for culture and arts in Belfast.

It started as a very humble society – putting on shows in St Mary's teacher training college, the Arts Theatre which is no more, the Ulster Hall and the Grand Opera House. The spring shows started around 30 years ago and there has been a show every year since, performing all the classical musical theatre. At the start of the Troubles people had to get to rehearsals through the bombs – the bombs at the Europa Hotel and the Grand Opera House.

There are major costs involved in our productions – hiring the Opera House, transporting sets from England for example. We hire professional tutors, dancers, choreographers and a professional director from London to bring the members up to speed and to a very high standard – that's required when you go into a major professional venue like the Grand Opera House.

St Agnes' is run by a committee of nine, all volunteers. There are many people who help us purely as volunteers. Collecting props is a major exercise. There are so many small things needed – like pocket watches, lamps, hand held props. There is a lady called the Props Mistress who scours around Belfast for props. The director gives her a list of what's needed and she goes off and does it.

Grand Opera House
with new extension,
2007, courtesy Grand
Opera House

October 23rd

St Agnes Choral Society in
"THE MAGIC OF THE MUSICALS"
with Guests
Subscription £12.00
(Concession £10.00)

St Agnes'
CHORAL SOCIETY

The
PHANTOM
of the
OPERA

Les
Misérables

Fiddler
on the Roof

CATS

Our Patron's Secretary is a past star of the shows, now retired. We have over 100 patrons. She writes to them, sends out application forms for tickets. This is all done from her own home on her own computer. It's a major exercise that she takes on as a volunteer.

Children are brought in by their parents and they all have chaperones who are vetted to work with children. We are privileged to have half a dozen school teachers but the documents still have to be done by volunteers, the forms filled in and processed.

It's voluntary, voluntary, voluntary – they are outstanding volunteers.

I'm mad about musical theatre – I just love it.

I'm retired but I don't want to put on my slippers yet. From 7 to 10.30pm night after night – it's aggressive rehearsals. You get tired sometimes, but if I sit down and put my slippers on, that's the end of it.

I thought we could get it going here so I went to Belfast City Council, but to pull it off we had to be an organisation.

That's when Beyond Skin was started - to facilitate screenings of 1 Giant Leap. We got some funding from the Community Relations Council, Belfast City Council, Arts & Business and other groups and put on three cinema style screenings in a Belfast cinema plus two discussion forums.

We were able to bring the whole 1 Giant Leap band over – 12 of them – from Pakistan, South America, Israel – for a fortnight! I think we bit off more than we could chew at the time. I hadn't thought that far ahead but was passionate to get it screened.

After the 1 Giant Leap events we decided to invite musicians representing different cultures and living in Belfast into recording studios to create a CD called Motion – as in moving forward. The CD was released in February 2006. It involved 42 musicians from 11 countries. However I didn't think beyond that – I'm not too good at strategy.

I had a full time job with Concern Worldwide. I decided to give up the job to set up Beyond Skin as a charity, along with the Motion project. Since 2006 we have had 63 musicians from 19 countries touring around Northern Ireland. We have put on 172 events last year – in 42 schools.

The Motion Project is about cultural education. It includes artists, musicians and people who are gifted in other ways. We are open to ideas from the people we work with.

The radio station started in April 2008. It's called 'Homely Planet' and is an inter-cultural radio planet. It is broadcast online only – www.homelyplanet.org. It allows us to keep in touch with people we're working with all around the world and locally.

The Beyond Skin ethos is about getting people involved no matter what their abilities are – they

We're heavily involved in arts, and believe it's important to promote arts here rather than promote ourselves as an organisation.

can help with recording radio programmes, going out to schools or youth groups, or talking to politicians.

Beyond Skin is not against mainstream media or what religious groups believe. With political correctness people are afraid to ask questions. We need to address racism and sectarianism – to have debates, organise and create an environment where people from different cultural backgrounds can engage in culture, art, music, challenging racist attitudes, fear and understanding.

We make programmes about religion, about peace and reconciliation. We are proud of it.

We were forced to set up as a limited company – Motion2Music. It struggled its way through a funding crisis – you need to know how to survive on your own. Our events, initiatives, the radio station are all designed to be self sufficient.

We're heavily involved in arts, and believe it's important to promote arts here rather than promote ourselves as an organisation. It's more important that we promote the issues.

Our volunteers are passionate about what they do. We have an amazing team of people and networks throughout Northern Ireland who are both skilled and passionate.

JENNIE McCULLOUGH *Bruised Fruit*

'I volunteer for Bruised Fruit, an organisation staffed fully by volunteers. Based in Belfast, it provides support for the music industry by supporting local groups. I got into volunteering through a guy who was working on a musical. I got into producing for a year and met a whole pile of musicians. They were complaining that they had nowhere to put on gigs. No one was interested in unsigned bands. We started weekly club nights for local bands, and from that people started asking us to do more things. The company Bruised Fruit was formed from that. It has always been run by volunteer staff providing support for local bands, to help them to further their careers.

One of the things that changed direction for us most was when Gary Lightbody from Snow Patrol came into one of our gigs one night and asked me to get more involved in setting up a record label. That was about two years ago and has been life changing for the company. He had heard what we were doing for local bands and came out of the blue. It was very exciting and a bit unexpected. That was one of the moments that stand out for me.

We get little bits of funding here and there. It allows us to take on bigger jobs for example with the BBC or with music festivals and sustains the work we do for free with bands who don't have any money.

If I could sum up volunteering in three words it would be varied, inspiring and for me, rewarding. I've got eight volunteers who support me and allow us to move forward.

The drive for me is supporting the other volunteers on the team,

Gary Lightbody (Snow Patrol) and Jonathan Wallace (Olympic Lifts) with Jennie McCullough from Bruised Fruit.

watching them benefit and develop. The reason I got involved with musicians was to help me build up experience for my own CV so I could apply for a job. But things changed. I was asked to do more things. Every so often I would get frustrated and say I'm going to apply for a job. Then I think I have worked up something that's of use to other people.

We work with 250 bands every year, with three or four people in each band – that's a thousand people a year we're giving a chance to.

It's become a part of so many people's lives – to help them get on stage and have a chance to play their music. When you look at it in those terms it's quite remarkable, and to think that it started with me in my bedroom. '

> *If I could sum up volunteering in three words it would be varied, inspiring and for me, rewarding.*

JOHN KINDNESS *Artist*

The Big Fish by John Kindness, now an iconic Belfast landmark, Arts Council of Northern Ireland.

' The year prior to the UHU group, 1972, I operated as an individual travelling arts and crafts person. I had art materials ironically in an old ammunition box which had been painted white and covered in symbols unrelated to war.

I travelled around play schemes doing arts activities with kids. It was felt to be successful, and was decided next year to start up a group – with four other people and a van – this became UHU.

The Quakers were one of the first groups to involve themselves in setting up play schemes. Then the play schemes started to attract a lot of international volunteers – they came from a lot of different places to help, even Australia. Other countries started to feel sympathy for the kids in Northern Ireland struggling to make sense of their disintegrating social order.

We had a van and were able to carry a lot of materials and expand activities. We could be working with groups of around twelve, or sometimes up to sixty or seventy – it sometimes became quite massive. We would take on a theme – we did pirates, and had a big bag of off-cuts of dyed sheepskin which made fantastic beards and moustaches.

Another time the group came up with a red Indian theme. The kids got totally caught up in this. It was good but chaotic. Our visits were memorable. There were a lot of volunteers with no expertise in arts and crafts, they came from completely different backgrounds.

It brought me to a lot of different areas of Belfast. Although communities were cautious as they were under threat, the Play Schemes were a good way to be inside neighbourhoods at war with each other, and we might be visiting their enemies the next day. Someone from another planet wouldn't understand the sectarian division in Belfast or recognise two different cultures, and I believe that most of the division is imaginary – these communities didn't realise that they were 99 per cent the same because they never interacted with each other.

There was a disused railway playground near Botanic Station, which didn't exist then, and we chiselled carvings in the sandstone. They might be still there.

Some activities had two purposes. For example, we would pick up broken glass from the playground and there was always a lot of it, and turn it into mosaics on the walls using tile cement and grout. Community art wasn't a term we used. I always thought if I'd to define real community art in Northern Ireland it was dangerous and sectarian, but extremely vibrant – all the traditional trappings of Orangeism and the then new Republican wall murals. There was a tendency when the authorities or people like the Arts Council got involved, to try and sanitise everything – to bring in the clowns. '

BILLY CAMPBELL *Youth Action and Fleming Fulton*

I went to Fleming Fulton and left in 1970. I was in the PHAB Club - it started there with Susan Harrison. Margaret O'Neill was the leader and organiser. During this time Children's Community Holidays were looking to get some disabled people involved. I was one of the people who went and got involved, and did a four day training course. The next year, we took children from 14 to 18 away on a week's holiday to Kilkeel.

The training course gave us techniques to entertain children for a week, techniques to get them to enjoy the holiday. If you get them in the right atmosphere, teenage kids can be really good. When in the right frame of mind, most joined in.

I was a member of the Board of the Northern Ireland Association of Youth Clubs – now called Youth Action. That was way back in the seventies. Before I was on the Board, they ran a course for young unemployed people and people at risk. It was called McAllister Brew course at the very beginning and then it changed its name to Young People at Work. It was a long time ago, way back in the seventies.

I went on the course – first of all as a participant, later I trained and became a volunteer for four or five years.

I found the course really inspiring to be on – even more inspiring to work on. I remember one fella when I worked on the course – he was very into himself. Each tutor worked with seven or eight young people in the group. In the training you were given techniques to get them to open up and talk. In my group this young fella – the first thing he did was pull up a few seats, put his feet up and fell asleep.

He didn't seem to like me because I was disabled. He was against certain types of people in the community. He made it clear that he didn't want to take part in anything.

Billy Campbell (third from right) at Hampton House, in the early days of the Northern Ireland Association of Youth Clubs – undertaking McAllister Brew training

On the second day it was the same. Then we got the group to talk about each other, how they reacted to each other, and that got him to open up about himself. The next day he started taking part. By the last day, he was great. He was able to open up, I asked the youth leader where he could go and talk about these problems he had. He walked out at the end of the course a totally different person (from) who had started on the Monday.

That was the most dramatic change in a person I'd ever seen.

When I was in a group like that, my job was not to say much – but to start something and let the group take over, and in some ways be a referee. That was way back in the seventies, but he will always stick out in my mind.

I went to the Art College and did a degree, so I drew back from work like that – but stayed on the

Board of PHAB in Fleming Fulton until the 1990s. I made a whole lot of friends.

I never stopped going to the school after I left. In the 1990's I would go in on a Friday afternoon and do some art with young people in their wheelchairs. They couldn't use their arms so we had to come up with something different. Over time we had an idea to do something a bit mad. We got two massive sheets of plastic, put one on the floor and covered it in paper. We found ways of splashing the paint, then covered it in more paper – it was about six foot squared. We then covered it with more plastic. The kids ran over it in their wheelchairs. It resulted in one big piece of art.

Painting was the only thing I could do. I couldn't write, I can't hold a pencil or a pen, so I used to type on an electric typewriter – I had to hold my hands together. I discovered I could type with my chin. I did it secretly – I thought the teachers wouldn't like me typing with my chin, but one saw me, and thought I could use my forehead.

Then a therapist thought about it and tied a paintbrush to a pointer, and that meant I could paint.

I was about 14. You know the way they get children to finger paint – they have not much control of their hands at first – I couldn't paint. I was awful. I could control the brush. I was encouraged at school, I would start painting. I went to the Isle of Man with the school. I had some pocket money left and mum and dad said 'why don't you buy some oil paints' so I did, and painted. I went into school with it – it was awful. They said it was great and asked me to do another one. When I took it in they said it was good, but not as good as the other one. I liked that, it gave me something to work towards.

I left school at 19. May Noble lived in Dunmurry in a big house. She was a volunteer with Fleming Fulton. She took the Brownies and the Guides. She got the Lagan Valley Round table to raise funds – and built this studio for me. The PHAB Club in Fleming Fulton started doing night classes in art. One of the teachers, Bill Sloan, encouraged me to go to Rupert

Stanley and do A level Art and O Level English. The students encouraged me to go on to the Polytechnic. I did a four year arts degree and a foundation year. Neil Shawcross was one of my tutors at the Art College – that's me in the eighties (*referring to an original Shawcross painting behind him, mounted on the wall*).

Nature reserve volunteers

Unlocking the Potential

The Trust's 'Unlocking the Potential' volunteer project is drawing to a close, so we thought this would be the right time to tell you what the project has achieved and what the future holds for volunteering at the Ulster Wildlife Trust.

Why the Ulster Wildlife Trust needed the project
Historically there was no member of staff dedicated to volunteering, which meant that volunteer policies and procedures were underdeveloped, there were no centralised records of volunteers, the public profile of volunteering was low, and a lack of funding meant things like expenses and training couldn't be offered to all volunteers.

Over two and half years ago we were successful in applying for a Community Volunteering Scheme (CVS) grant funded through the Department for Social Development. The project allowed the Trust to appoint a full-time Volunteering Officer dedicated to the development of volunteering.

Some of the core elements of the project were - to see an overall increase in the number of volunteers and the hours they put in; a much more diverse range of volunteers; ensuring volunteers benefitted from their involvement with the Trust; and that increased volunteer involvement enabled the Trust to reach its organisational goals. A major requirement of the project was to engage with sections of society that traditionally have been underrepresented in the voluntary sector, and to this end, we recruited volunteers who were long-term unemployed, had a physical or mental disability, were from an ethnic background and were aged under 25 and over 50.

The funding also meant that we were able to offer expenses, produce a wide variety of promotional materials from pens to postcards, offer volunteers branded clothing and produce a volunteer newsletter.

In early 2006, we were in a position to get out there and start recruiting volunteers - we recruited them from all walks of life and they helped with a wide range of roles.

Article from The Irish Hare *(The Ulster Wildlife Trust), Issue 91 –Spring 2009*

Volunteers – they come

Below is just a snapshot of some of th

We worked with a range of disability groups, these have included - Action Mental Health (New Horizons), the Cedar Foundation, Ravenhill Adult Centre and Woodstock Lodge - who all helped out across the Belfast reserves with a range of tasks from path clearance to litter lifts and bird box building.

New Horizons helping at Bog Meadows

The project attracted a variety of businesses who wanted to come out for a day onto a nature reserve for some 'team-building' and do something worthwhile for charity. These included Deloitte who helped create a giant bird table at Bog Meadows and Northern Bank who cleared that most invasive of invasive species Japanese knotweed. Most recently a group of 40 new recruits from the PSNI helped plant trees at Ecos Nature Park.

Northern Bank staff at Bog Meadows

The Trust has worked closely with young offenders over the past three years too. Through the Youth Conference Service, young people are asked to complete community hours rather than being given a custodial sentence. Initially, we were only offering opportunities to young people from the Greater Belfast area but over the course of the project we have been working with young people from Newtownabbey, Ballymena, Downpatrick and Bangor. Most young people have helped with practical tasks out on nature reserves.

n all shapes and sizes!

volunteers we work with.

During the project we have welcomed 11 people from across Europe on European Voluntary Service (EVS) placements – volunteers came from Germany, France, Italy, Spain and Poland. All made a vital contribution to all aspects of nature conservation; some went home with an NVQ, others with an Open College Network (OCN) certificate. It was always sad to see them leave but they all took away some fantastic memories, made lots of friends along the way and had lots of craic!

Agata and Dani - EVS Volunteers

Not all volunteers came on board to get involved in practical work on our nature reserves, a fair few came into the Crossgar office and got involved with administration duties and packing of the Irish Hare. Already in 2009, three new volunteers have come on board and are helping on reception.

Lucy helping at a Volunteer recruitment event

Other volunteers were given dedicated roles and helped our Fundraising and Communications Officer, our Key Species Officer and the Outreach and Learning team. Outside of Crossgar, volunteers were leading Wildlife Watch groups in Belfast and up at the Ecos Centre, and during the summer months there were volunteers helping on stands at events such as the Garden Festival at Hillsborough Castle.

Who has gained from the project?

In 1978 a group of enthusiastic and dedicated people got together to form the Ulster Trust for Nature Conservation (later changing their name to the Ulster Wildlife Trust). They were all volunteers and had seen a need to set up an organisation with expertise in nature conservation. 30 years on and volunteers are as important now as they were back in 1978. Without volunteers and their commitment, the Ulster Wildlife Trust wouldn't be half as strong as it is today!

It is fair to say that during the project both the Ulster Wildlife Trust and all the volunteers have benefitted in one form or other. We have used the skills, knowledge and expertise of a wide range of people to help deliver our aims and at the same time volunteers have learnt new skills, gained qualifications, had fun, made new friends and gone on to find work in the conservation sector. The funding has also allowed us to develop our policies and procedures so that we are now in a position to manage our volunteers efficiently and effectively.

Some amazing statistics

A summary of the project shows that over 50 volunteers gained an accredited qualification during their time volunteering with us. The most startling statistic to come out of the project is the number of hours that volunteers put in up to December 2008. They contributed 31380 hours which equates to a remarkable 4483 days. Also, we are well on our way to reaching the target of having 150 active volunteers on board by the end of the project.

What next?

The 'Unlocking the Potential' project has provided an opportunity for volunteering to become an even more effective resource in the Trust's work and it has also shown that volunteers are integral to our continued effectiveness and future success. It is also safe to say that volunteers are now recognised and rewarded more than at any other time during our history.

We would like to say a huge thank-you to all volunteers and staff who made the 'Unlocking the Potential' project such a success, especially Ian Cardwell who, as Volunteering Officer, played a key role in its delivery. Thanks also to the Volunteer Development Agency for all their support and the Department for Social Development which provided the funding.

Ian Cardwell

As of April 2009 we no longer have a full-time Volunteering Officer as the project funding has come to an end. However, volunteering has come on in leaps and bounds and is at the cornerstone of what the Ulster Wildlife Trust is about – engaging people in local nature conservation.

The project has enabled us to develop our volunteering systems and procedures so that our staff are well equipped for recruiting and managing volunteers into the future. The Ulster Wildlife Trust is committed to providing opportunities for volunteers in all of its areas of work, and will continue to value the impact that volunteers make on a daily basis.

Current opportunities

These are just some of the areas where we are currently seeking volunteers' help.
- Receptionist/Admin Volunteers – based at Crossgar – any time from half a day a week welcomed.
- Nature Reserves Volunteers – particularly Balloo in Bangor and Ecos in Ballymena.
- Wildlife Watch Leaders – help with a current group or set up a new one to teach young people about nature.

For further information on these or any other volunteering opportunities please visit our website, call us at our Crossgar office or email volunteering@ ulsterwildlifetrust.org.

MARGARET MARSHALL *Belfast Naturalists' Field Club*

' I'm now 75 and I've been a volunteer since I was a school girl. I was brought up in the country and was interested in wildflowers and birds. I joined Ulster Wildlife Trust – and volunteered in Glenarm Nature Reserve.

I went to Bog Meadows to plant willows with the UWT. John Wilde and Stan Beesley were working on their book the *Urban Flora of Belfast* which was published in 1997. I spent three years doing survey work as a member of the Belfast Naturalists' Field Club. They gave me kilometre squares to survey over two to three years. The Bog Meadows was one of the kilometre squares I surveyed. It doesn't sound like much – but we had to survey every street and avenue and note every plant we found. The most interesting square is the City Cemetery – it has several interesting plants. I was helped by John Wilde – who is now 89 and still out botanising. We traipsed all over Bog Meadows, and drew up a list of 180 or more plants.

My parents always encouraged voluntary work. People who volunteer learn that from their parents. I've always enjoyed the contact through volunteering.

The Bog Meadows – what's left – are preserved by the Ulster Wildlife Trust. They dug out ponds to encourage birds and ducks in winter. There are many unusual plants there.

The Friends of Bog Meadows has an office on the Falls Road – getting young boys and girls involved also at Colin Glen. They helped to clean it – to involved local young people – who are taking an interest in preserving it.

I have other volunteer interests. I've been a volunteer with Citizens Advice Bureau since 1993. The computer information system covers all sorts of

Surveying Belfast bit by bit, Margaret Marshall

problems – from common problems like benefits to how to get a 100th birthday card from the Queen – it's through the pensions branch.

You get very good training. CAB volunteers are all expected to do two sessions of four hours per week. The telephone never stops ringing – there are never enough people to answer it. A lot of people need help and some of the queries are quite complicated.

My queries are usually to do with benefits. It takes time to check out the information. Apart from the CAB, my other main interest for volunteering is Integrated Education.

I've been governor of four different schools and helped set up the Millennium Integrated School in Carryduff which opened in 2000. I'm still on the Board of Governors. '

> *The most interesting square is the City Cemetery – it has several interesting plants.*

PATSY HARBINSON

I became an RSPB volunteer in 2007. Although I was interested in wildlife generally, I went to Spain after university as part of a programme to learn Spanish. I had studied Zoology at Bangor University in Wales. My three month placement was at a bird rescue centre in Seville.

When I came back to Northern Ireland I thought about what I could do with the RSPB. Before the placement I liked birds but had no real interest in them. I worked as a volunteer at reception and dealing with general enquiries. The RSPB has a volunteer warden scheme and so I applied for Rathlin Island. I was only supposed to be there for two weeks but stayed for the summer. The main part of that role is helping people to see the birds and the puffins – explaining what the RSPB is and what it does.

It was great experience. I came back to Belfast and worked as a volunteer in the office. Then I got a job as an information assistant – showing people birds and looking after the volunteers.

In Belfast, at HQ there are always volunteers helping at events, doing summer surveys and field research. While at university I gave up some time to volunteer – it's essential for me to volunteer. It was a revelation to me as I got older.

It is such a broad field – volunteering helped me find out what it is I want to do. I work closely now with the volunteer development officer. The organisation has a background steeped in volunteering.

It's my belief in the need to care for the environment that has drawn me to the RSPB. Being an RSPB volunteer is an important part of a larger picture. I relate easily to the volunteers – there are so many different types of volunteers.

STEPHEN HARRIS

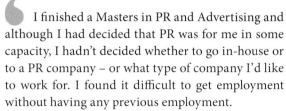

I finished a Masters in PR and Advertising and although I had decided that PR was for me in some capacity, I hadn't decided whether to go in-house or to a PR company – or what type of company I'd like to work for. I found it difficult to get employment without having any previous employment.

I applied for jobs, but had no experience. On the Community NI website I noticed that the RSPB was looking for volunteers. The biggest draw for me was to gain PR experience.

It never occurred to me I'd end up working in an organisation concerned with wildlife. I had considered working for a charity or an NGO – they provide different challenges and opportunities to meet people, and it's more than just doing PR for a company where you have to flit between different clients. This suited me much better – I could get my teeth into it.

I certainly wouldn't say I'm any type of expert, but I know considerably more about birds now. I came as a lay-man, not with a conservation or bird watching background. In some ways that might have been an advantage for me in my role. I'm dealing with the public – and if I find it interesting, then it's generally an interesting story – like the Red Kite launch.

The Red Kite story has been one of our great success stories. I was a volunteer during the Red Kite launch, which was amazing. It inspired a lot of people – people who were not necessarily into birds. It was a great PR story and it was inspiring to see a species re-introduced.

JIM McKEOWN *Belfast Zoo*

'Being a volunteer at the zoo is me giving my bit back to the community. It's a beautiful location, so many exotic animals – and I love making life easier for them and enhancing the enclosures for the public.

Enclosure work means the animals are happy and content. The volunteers also raise funds for the species and conservation aspect, and look after the zoological gardens – to help safeguard the gardens for future generations.

It's good for the soul to get away from the madness of society.

I've been a volunteer at the zoo for seven or eight years now. One day I asked one of the keepers about being a volunteer, and he advised me to contact the Friends of the Zoo. We sell tickets, sell badges – help to fundraise.

Occasionally the volunteers get close to the animals – but it's well supervised and organised. It's great to get behind the scenes with the gorillas

Jim with Johti the elephant

and the bears – I have some lovely photographs of elephants and giraffes. Occasionally through the kids club my kids get close to the animals – we can get access that the public don't. We can get right up close to the cage – to see the animal, smell it – to get more of a grasp of its size, the noises it makes.

The voluntary work is mostly out in the enclosures doing the work, and at the end of the day, when they let the animals back in, it's great to watch them investigate what's been done – maybe a new climbing frame, or finding some food that's been left for them. It's nice for the animals and it's nice for us.'

AGENTS FOR CHANGE

Lower Ormeau mothers and children. Photo: Brian Greene

AT ONE TIME
A personal reflection by Fionnuala O'Connor

In the pre-Troubles years, May Blood jokes, volunteering meant no more than helping your neighbour. The word "volunteer" came later, she says, and later still grants, red tape and controversy. May Blood was a trade union activist for decades in disheartened loyalist districts, then a member of the now dissolved Women's Coalition. She was made a baroness at the suggestion of the late Mo Mowlam, who as Northern Ireland Secretary clearly favoured a supporter of the emerging peace process, and of volunteering – which many local women always chose over male-dominated party politics. A well-meant jest about the Women's Coalition was that they were really community groups in new guise.

Over the past forty years much volunteering, from organising protests or choirs to meals-on-wheels for the elderly, has of course resembled that elsewhere. For many it has also meant extraordinary pressure: working reluctantly alongside or entwined with paramilitaries, being wooed or denounced, sometimes both in turn, by agencies of church and state. As the last pretence of order and normal politics was replaced by criminality and near-anarchy in

parts of Belfast, volunteering gained significance but struggled to keep its feet. Mending the damage of the Troubles may need fresh activists for a new era.

It is hard to re-create the feel of pre-Troubles Northern Ireland. Some like to suggest that a sweet old-fashioned place was swept away by violence. But there were no widely accepted civic norms: this was not one society, but two. As campaigns against Catholic disadvantage in the fractious late 1960s began to be matched by Protestant reaction, strong personalities came to the fore in various spheres. Civil rights agitation could be described as one dramatic and influential form of volunteer activity, its opposite the array of unionist pressure groups: both in the end were largely absorbed into the political/paramilitary maelstrom. (John Hume, Gerry Adams and Anna Lo all describe themselves as initially civic activists rather than party political animals.) A spread of individuals and the enterprises they generated dug in through decades of upheaval, May Blood among them.

The Troubles brought volunteering – in the sense of working without payment, with and for your neighbours at their behest – into the front line. With policing and government locked in combat to greater or lesser degree against a section of one community, while the other demanded that no quarter be given, volunteers tried to pick up the pieces. Citizens defence committees of all sorts sprang up, many evolving into paramilitaries. Most groups which campaign today for the bereaved or injured began with people offering others support or lobbying authority at their own expense. When families became homeless in the midst of gunfire and intimidation it was volunteers who found lorries, drove their possessions, opened schools as refuges, cooked and provided clothing.

Some went on to campaign against poor housing, the sewage system that caused dysentery in Moyard flats, the "Weetabix" flats on the Shankill. Some became paramilitaries, and/or worked to support paramilitary prisoners and their families. Ex-loyalist prisoner Billy Mitchell worked with ex-republican internee Liam Maskey to reduce friction in north Belfast. By that stage volunteering had been increasingly absorbed into official conflict-management, with funding for organisers who could prove they were "cross-community." But loyalists failed to make the leap from violence and crime into politics that the IRA made into Sinn Fein.

Some who have volunteered, and also been paid, find it easier than others to assess developments because of their own backgrounds, and their location in the bigger picture. Maurice Hayes was one of the first to deal with volunteers across the city's divide. Like John Hume, a long-time friend, he came from a generation that saw the Catholic community damaged by frustration and impotence, and argued for participation – civic volunteering - as the way to make changes. He remained an Irish language and GAA enthusiast. He also became a senior civil servant, drafted much of the Patten report on police reform, and for over 20 years was chair of the Ireland Funds' grants committee.

In December 1969 he was that rare animal, a Catholic willing to take a public post from the unionist government of the day: as first chair

Waiting to be searched, Lower Ormeau Road. Photo: Brian Greene

of the Community Relations Commission (CRC), set up at the onset of unrest. His memoir "Minority Verdict" describes an attempt to create "a sense of shared citizenship" against the grain of social and other services organised on denominational lines. "Field workers" in Belfast included community workers from both sides of the then-new peaceline. It was easier to work with Catholics, Hayes writes: Protestants tended to see the Commission as a sop to civil righters, while Catholics regarded community development as a channel for energies released by civil rights.

When several hundred men and youths were arrested on the morning of August 9th 1971 and "interned" without charge, none on suspicion of involvement with loyalist paramilitarism, Belfast went up in flames. When names of internees emerged the CRC field workers "recoiled in anger and horror… many were voluntary community workers who had been encouraged by our intervention to put their heads above the parapet and point people towards new and peaceful paths." A third of the internees were released within days, as having no involvement with the IRA.

Bomb blast, Lower Ormeau Road. Photo: Brian Greene

The comparative peace of the past ten years, with communities losing the cohesion of fear and shared purpose, has been tough on volunteering. It has lost its "first abandon," Hayes jokingly agrees, to some degree becoming regimented. With characteristic optimism he hopes that as funding for paid workers disappears in the recession, newcomers may volunteer. It could even, he thinks, be a rebirth.

Maggie Beirne is not so sure: she sees a modern culture which emphasises earning money "rather than donating time." After 17 years with Amnesty International she joined the Committee on the Administration of Justice (CAJ) initially as a volunteer (like some current staff) and helped win it international respect – for its "fire-fighting" in the worst of the Troubles – and later work on criminal justice, equality, policing and protection of rights.

She became director in 2004, and left Belfast in 2008 for more volunteering in London, her birthplace. The level of Northern Ireland activity still impresses her. She has no doubt about its origins. "It attracted 'political' people who wanted to make a difference and bring about change but knew that affiliation to either unionism or nationalism would restrict them. If one cares about autism, children in care, elderly healthcare, anti-racism, there is little advantage to be gained in being overly associated with one or other side of the constitutional question, and limiting one's options for cross-cutting alliances."

But in the following weeks at least 2,000 Belfast families and possibly 2,500, according to one official estimate, twice as many of them Catholic as Protestant, left their homes after threats or actual violence. Internment and its consequences sent the first official attempt to co-opt grassroot energies crashing off the rails. It would be increasingly difficult to do anything of the sort in the breakdown of state and society that followed, the Hayes account correctly notes.

His career since – particularly as chair of the Ireland Fund's grant committee – has taken Hayes through the period when "community worker" became a cynical euphemism, with many groups dominated, for better or worse, by the strongest local paramilitary force. (The lowest point may have been the "Community House" in the lower Shankill where UDA boss Mad Dog Johnny Adair – he relished the nickname – liked to be interviewed.) But Hayes has always argued that many ex-paramilitaries brought energy to voluntary work and then funded groups, becoming a powerful element in the turnaround that eventually left violence behind.

> *She sees a distinction between volunteers on "justice issues" and "charity volunteers."*

A modest person, almost painfully scrupulous, Beirne like her colleagues from the start faced unionist conviction that the "human rights agenda" of the CAJ was intrinsically pro-republican. Official attitudes dismayed her, "the political vetting and channelling of government money to west Belfast via the Catholic church" to avoid it going to anyone of whom officials did not approve. "Professional bias fed a political agenda that wanted to engage in social engineering". But segregation, and the dominance of different politics in different areas, certainly made it difficult for volunteers to reach across the divide. "I know of some loyalist groups that started to reach out to republican areas and officials to share information and campaign tips – in the belief that the Catholics knew best how to work the system! This required a lot of courage, as well as honesty."

She sees a distinction between volunteers on "justice issues" and "charity volunteers." The first are "more attracted to working with non-governmental organisations for the elderly, insisting on improved benefits, on people participating to improve their own situation rather than doing things for them: charity volunteers are more likely to want to visit old people in their homes, decorating etc."

As for a balance between paid staff and effective use of volunteers, few organisations get that right, she says. "It is a constant problem, not peculiar to Northern Ireland or funding arrangements

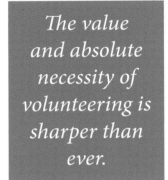

The value and absolute necessity of volunteering is sharper than ever.

here, that volunteers get squeezed out once money starts to arrive." Looking back from London, Beirne is inclined to think that whatever the level of volunteering, those who "look for justice" for the deprived or aggrieved may still tend to meet something like the reaction recorded by Helder Camara, the campaigning Brazilian archbishop who died ten years ago: "When I give food to the poor, they call me a saint. When I ask why the poor have no food, they call me a Communist."

Baroness May Blood lives in west Belfast's Springmartin estate, where she moved with her parents two years into the Troubles. Cheerful and realistic, she is downbeat about voluntary sector development since her first involvement as a trade unionist mill-worker around her birthplace: long-gone Magnetic Street, now covered by the Westlink. "It would be called a mixed area now – it was the focus of daily rioting for almost two years. We tried to instill into people to stick together as a community."

Then she campaigned against the dereliction of the Springmartin estate, split between UDA and UVF. A residents' association survived for only six months. Yes, she says, organisation came more naturally in Catholic districts. "They felt they had to do it for themselves, there's no doubt there was discrimination there." But a 'Black Mountain Action group' established itself. Kate Kelly of the Belfast Action Team was "a godsend. She got us a disused flat as an office and our first grant – £67." Through entirely voluntary work they raised £46,000 and agreed a five year development plan, including funds for a paid worker. "And volunteering finished – people said the worker's being paid to do it. Be careful what you wish for."

City Hall peace rally. Photo: Brian Greene

Blood at 71 is still driving around Belfast and beyond to raise funds for integrated education and speak at meetings on community development, on top of involvement in Shankill early childhood intervention schemes and attendance in the Lords. She is shocked that friends with comfortable pensions are unwilling to volunteer, though others still contribute without financial reward. A friend in Rathcoole could not paint her house over a weekend because he was coaching one children's football team after another. Typical enough of football, and boxing, says Blood, sustained by volunteers, "never any real money into either."

What happens when grants dry up and the salaries can no longer be paid? "Money was thrown at us to keep us quiet, millions into the Shankill and unfortunately not much to show for it. Most went by the board."

With official funding about to be scarcer than for a long time, the plight of many areas could well get worse instead of better. There are still many affected by poor housing provision, poverty, ill-health, lack of skills and education - and unemployment, with its corrosive effect on a person's sense of self, is soaring. The value and absolute necessity of volunteering is sharper than ever.

BARONESS MAY BLOOD *Community Activist*

'I was brought up off the Grosvenor Road. We were poor but I didn't know we were poor. We enjoyed ourselves and did things ourselves – street parties, that sort of thing.

I was a volunteer from an early age – but didn't consider it that, it was just what you did.

When I worked at the Mill I was involved in helping people. I was nosey and that helped me. The sixties was a boom time for textiles – people were getting carpet on their floors for the first time instead of lino.

If a woman was having a baby, everyone clubbed around. If there was a death, everyone rallied round. I grew up in that spirit. My mother and father both worked – my mother would have made extra food and taken it down to others who didn't have.

In the late sixties the Civil Rights movement started. It was the first time I thought there were people worse off than us. There was talk about the IRA but that died down. Then in '69 the whole thing exploded in rioting. Volunteers were needed to calm things – to prevent fighting between Catholics on the Falls Road and Protestants on the Sandy Row.

In the next few years, the whole district disintegrated.

We were forced to move into what was a loyalist ghetto. That was very hard. The estate was a mess and needed cleared up. We set up a voluntary group – all women, and one man – he was good at writing letters. We started challenging people. We were told that if we wanted to make a real difference we would have to come up with a five year plan.

Business in the Community was set up in the early eighties and that was the first time we ever made contact with professional people. There was a group of women working with the Catholic community on the other side

of a thirty foot wall. They had the same problems. We started writing letters.

I had a trade union background which was invaluable. It allowed me to chair meetings, to challenge. We got a one bed flat from the Housing Executive and started to make and take complaints. We started to see that five year plan roll out.

In the late '80s the Belfast Action Team opened offices and were giving out grants. We had meetings in our own homes on Sunday afternoons – you just did what you had to do. The BAT leader said there were certain grants we could apply for. The women said 'we're not looking for money – just ordinary things like clean streets.'

The volunteers didn't want to handle money. They felt that money would change the whole psychology of the group.

In the '90s there was much to be done. The issues were things like benefits, housing, health. When the Black Mountain Action Group got its first grant from Belfast City Council

THE
RAPE AND PLUNDER
OF THE SHANKILL
IN BELFAST

PEOPLE AND
PLANNING

by Ron Wiener

THE RAPE & PLUNDER OF THE SHANKILL

COMMUNITY ACTION:
the Belfast experience

Book published in 1975

it was for £67. We thought we owned the Shore Road. It was just for stamps and letters. Our five year plan took ten years to roll out.

I had been a volunteer all my life but in 1991 I became a paid worker. As a volunteer I was making a contribution, as a paid worker I was doing a job.

Now some say 'why should I give that, or do this – sure the government will do that.' But there is a lesson – the money is running out. Volunteers are the biggest and best resource we have in the community.

In 1990 the Mill closed. I was unemployed for the first time in my life. For eight months I did purely voluntary work, but there was something missing in my life.

The Greater Shankill Strategy Partnership was set up in 1993. The Board was entirely made up of volunteers.

From 1993 on I became a paid worker here, but it showed me how we were losing the power of volunteering. There is an edge to volunteering, you do it because you want to be there – it's not a job of work.

> *The House of Lords is one of the hardest working places. I thought it was full of dusty old men, but I got my eyes opened.*

My volunteering background started in trade unionism. In 1967 I became a shop steward. My father was a strong trade unionist – but he was opposed to women being shop stewards. He was not happy about his own daughter being one. I went on to be a senior shop steward, and got a lot of free education. It enabled me to study law, negotiation skills, public speaking.

I went to a conference in Boston in 1994. There were 32 of us from the North and 20 from the South. I came away believing that women were the people in Northern Ireland who could change it from within.

I was one of the founder members of the Women's Coalition in 1996. It had two women elected to the Assembly, while a group of women were working their socks off to make it work.

In 1999 I was elected into the House of Lords. It was a senior civil servant put me forward to the Prime Minister. I accepted the offer after some hesitation – I said 'no' at first. Then I thought about the women who were not being given opportunities.

I had no idea what I was getting into.

People generally don't know that in Westminster there are thousands and thousands of volunteers all working for the good of the country. The House of Lords is one of the hardest working places. I thought it was full of dusty old men, but I got my eyes opened.

I am also passionate about integrated education. I'm chair of the Integrated Education Fund and fundraise all over the world. It's amazing that no matter where I travel people are interested in what we're doing. The integrated

Hammer Playground, Shankhill Road, 1970s

movement is different. Parents and volunteers run it all.

The IEF couldn't exist without volunteers – so many organisations couldn't exist without volunteers. It's something we have to get back to. There is a buzz with groups of volunteers that you don't get with paid workers.

Volunteers will chip in with their talents – some can bake cakes, or set tables – or say 'I can do this or that'. With volunteering, everyone is as valued as the next person.

I think more women volunteer than men. There were groups of women who made the Peace Quilt and took it up to Stormont. There was a great buzz in that room, you could hear the excitement in their voices – that the quilt was not the end, just the beginning.

Women do and can do so much – during the Shankill feuds, it was the women who marched down the road and said 'not in my name'. Women can challenge, create change, network and empower.

It is amazing what women can do when they want to – there are so many amazing women in these communities. Their volunteer stories are never recorded and so many will be forgotten. We need the truth about these volunteers to be told. These communities would have gone over the edge without the tireless work of volunteers. In those days, they were taking real risks.

All over Northern Ireland there are stories of good minded volunteers who didn't want their communities to slip into anarchy. It was not fashionable to go across the peace line – but they did.

Cityweek, 18th July 1968

ANNE WALKER *Ballybeen Women's Centre*

'It was the local community worker who came up with the idea for a women's centre, somewhere for the women to get together and volunteer, to help each other out. We opened our women's centre in a wee room in Ballybeen Square.

Some students designed it for us – it was just a room within the basement of some flats. There would have been a lot of paramilitaries about back then, but this was a strong community.

It was just a drop-in centre to give the women a break. We had a few toys and each mother would mind the children for half an hour while we did things, like yoga.

As the women got stronger in themselves, they realised they were ready and prepared to learn. We wanted more opportunities for learning.

In 1989 we moved into our own building. At the very beginning the council paid the wages of the manager, and everything and anything else was done by volunteers. We were getting good results – we got the work done.

It was great to get somewhere of our own. At the beginning we had a hard time – even convincing our husbands. Some of the men felt threatened by this 'women's centre'. Some were afraid that their wives were getting out more and starting to learn more. A lot of husbands weren't wild about it, including my own.

I loved it here. It was fantastic watching the women who just called in for a cup of coffee, starting to come out of themselves. After a few weeks they'd get involved and start doing some courses. Quite a few went on to university and got degrees.

The women themselves wanted to do more and to get more courses organised. It was really starting to take off by the mid-1990s.

Our core priority was a commitment to the principles of community participation and empowerment. As more and more women were progressing through courses – word was getting out and about – and still all the women were volunteers.

I'd been a volunteer here for seventeen years. The Women's Centre had now become a part of me. I was out and about mentoring people, trying to encourage them to get involved.

The men didn't really like it. You had to know what life was like back then and the way we were brought up. Women were in the house getting everything ready. I was of that era. Some of the women were harder to convince, but this was about self-esteem and confidence. Now as the years go by, women are more independent. They go out and learn and earn.

My own children have come through this centre. My daughter and grand-daughter have done courses. It gave them something that I had learnt and valued – having an opinion, and respecting other people's opinions.

My children are quite proud of their mum now. I went to Washington DC as a representative of East Belfast. That was in 1993. I met President Clinton in the White House.

I went to the World Congress of Women in Moscow as part of a North-South delegation of women. It was 1986 and Russia was just starting to open out. Kruschev gave the keynote address – the conference was held in the Kremlin. There were four and a half thousand women from eighty different countries, yet everyone wanted to meet the women from Northern Ireland.

Especially the German women – they nearly fell off their seats when we told them that the women's centres in Belfast work with each other, no matter what part of the city they were in. At that time there was only about seven or eight women's centres, but we worked with each other and shared information. It's hard for people to realise that all this good work was being done by volunteers, and the majority were women.

We're really lucky in Ballybeen. We have our own management committee – mostly made up of older women, and they would do anything for you.

For me there is a thrill in watching women getting their certificates, and thinking, 'I helped her to do that', and hearing them say 'Oh My God I passed!'

This has been a totally life enriching experience for me. Years ago, I would never even have thought of doing a course, now through the centre I've done courses in Child Psychology, the Pre-School Child, English, history. I always felt I'd missed out on education because I was very young when my mum died.

Who would have thought that years later, I'd go to Washington – to the White House – as the representative from East Belfast. I'd think – this is me – Anne Walker, going to Moscow to represent East Belfast. That's just a part of what volunteering did for me – it showed me another world, a whole new world. ,

UNHEARD VOICES.

Women's Needs in Ardoyne

A Report by the Ardoyne Women's Research Project

LES ALLANBY *NI Law Centre*

' I was a student in Durham University and had no idea what I wanted to do when I finished. It was 1980 and I thought I could spend a year in Belfast and dine out on it for the next twenty-five years. I had no connection whatsoever with VSB. Those were the days of the Long Term Volunteers. Looking back, I am embarrassed at the level of youthful arrogance. I turned up for the interview with a briefcase and two suitcases and asked if I could leave them there over the weekend while I looked around for somewhere to stay. The idea of turning up now with suitcases would seem so arrogant!

As luck would have it, I was offered the post and had a few days to go around estate agents and knocking on doors looking for somewhere to live. I started with VSB on the Social Security rate plus £2 – it was £25 per week. I was one of three LTV's and worked with almost 9,000 volunteers for a year. Over the next year my job included organising gardening and decorating services for older people. They would provide the materials, I'd supervise the work.

I got involved with Belfast Housing Aid and developed an interest in the legal aspect of the Housing Rights Service NI. It was there that I first came into contact with the Law Centre. It was set up in 1977 and was very small – with four staff and a couple of volunteers – local lawyers, trade unionists and community workers.

So I found the work for VSB to be great experience. The people were warm and friendly. It was under Sydney Stewart at that time and he took me under his wing. He was an interesting character and VSB was very important to him, he was youthful and enthusiastic.

In July 1981 I went back to Durham to head up the student community action group I'd been involved in. I spent a year at that but I missed Belfast – it

was volatile at the time. The political background was that the second Hunger Strike had just reached its conclusion. The first Hunger Strike finished in December 1980, the second Hunger Strike was really from March 1981 and was called off at the end of July or August 1981. It was a time of great political volatility and was a fascinating time on one level to be in Belfast. Ironically I had thought I could have dined out for 25 years on my time in Belfast, but I missed the place. I liked the city and the people I got on well with.

I wrote to the Law Centre and asked if they would take me on as a volunteer – that was July 1982. I started as a volunteer on the Benefits Uptake Campaign, doing housing advice work.

After a year I got a full time job with the law centre. That same week I got a letter from the DHSS saying that I was not entitled to social security as I wasn't seeking work. That was in 1983, and I'm still here – 25 years later. '

ROMANA KHAOURY *Refugee Action Group (RAG)*

'My name is Romana Khaouy, at the moment I'm writing up my PhD in education policy, additionally I sit on the management board of the Multi Cultural Resource Centre – a local black and minority ethnic community organisation (part of the Bryson Charitable Group). I started volunteering when I began my under-graduate degree at Queen's University.

I came to Northern Ireland from Zimbabwe as a recently married woman. When I arrived in Belfast I remember feeling very isolated especially coming from a place where I had loads of family and friends. Therefore, I decided to keep myself busy and so I started studying in a local college which had a crèche attached, my daughter at the time had just turned two years old (the facility was a life-saver).

Through one of the students at the college I heard about the Multi-Cultural Centre and decided I would attend the Centre on Wednesday mornings to a mother and toddler type of group. I found that time very rewarding and made some life-long friends that I still keep in touch with today. The project was important especially for newly arrived isolated mums such as me. Two years later, I finished college and started a degree in Law and Policy at Queen's University – at that time I was interested in refugee law and policy and wanted to learn more about the practical issues regarding asylum seekers and refugees in the north of Ireland.

Around that time, the Multi-Cultural Resource Centre had begun an 'informal' project for asylum seekers and was set up by a collection of interested stake holders from various organisations – we called ourselves the Refugee Action Group. I approached the centre and asked if I could volunteer on the project and that's how I got involved with mainly visiting asylum seekers in Maghaberry Prison. The Refugee Action Group at that time worked in liaison with the Northern Ireland Law Centre and other organisations such as Amnesty International and the Human Rights Commission.

After a rigorous police check and some training from a visiting group in England, I started to visit the immigration detainees at Maghaberry. Some of the people we visited had no contacts in Belfast so we were a kind of visiting group providing company for them and others. Additionally, as a group we would ensure the detainees received medical attention or legal representation, at times we were allowed to bring reading literature in and food stuffs too. Some refugees and asylum seekers couldn't eat the food in prison due to their dietary requirements and we were authorised to bring with us parcels of food such as rice and bread – that were kindly donated from a large super market chain. Amnesty and the press helped raise awareness too. In conjunction with the

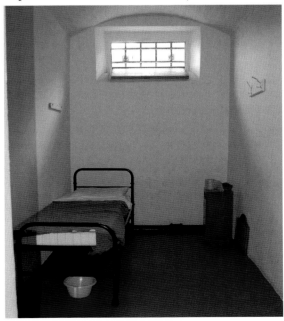

Cell in Crumlin Road Gaol, Belfast

National Union of Journalists we launched various documents on the media representation of refugee and asylum seekers along with reports highlighting the plights of the detainees and refugees.

Additionally, some of my case work involved visiting the families who predominately were living in Belfast (usually, families and children were held on the outside while the male head was detained).I would assist when asked in finding schools or doctors for these family members through various other agencies and service providers too.

At the start of my volunteering time prison visits began in Maghaberry, immigration detainees were previously housed in Magilligan Prison, consequently they were moved to the women's wing in Maghaberry and subsequently the men were sent to Crumlin Road Prison and the women to Hydebank Young Offenders Unit.

As a mother, dealing with families was very hard, sometimes I couldn't switch off – I'm not a tap in that sense. I would often be asked by detainees to 'get me out of here – I've done nothing bad, please get me out of here'; other times I faced scorn by the detainees who saw us as having very little say in their release (this was expected). Nevertheless, we were trying to liaise with the prison authorities and detainees and never had any major problems other than trying to get the detainees out as soon as possible. In fact I attended a detainee's wedding in Crumlin Road Jail – there were some pleasant moments at times, so to speak. Moreover, there was empathy, from a vast majority of people I dealt with and there was amazing goodwill too, as we also would work in partnership with other organisations like St Vincent de Paul and the Red Cross.

The visits were heartbreaking at times too. I remember a young Romanian boy with very blue eyes crying, he said 'I have done nothing wrong'. He didn't understand why he

Crumlin Road Gaol, Belfast

was imprisoned. The authorities were not satisfied he was here legally – but he had a genuine reason to seek refuge and was entitled to under the law too.

The one man, for me that I will never forget was a father from Kosovo I used to visit. His son was a few months old when he was detained. When they released him in court – nearly 10 months later I remembered the moment like it was yesterday, his son walking straight into his arms for the very first time.

Another harrowing time I recall is when I held a baby in my arms in court while his mother was taken to Hydebank. I was told she could not hold her baby, the authorities feared the lady would not let the baby go, so she held his hand through the bars.

> *As a mother, dealing with families was very hard, sometimes I couldn't switch off – I'm not a tap in that sense.*

The baby had his dad to return to, but I was very concerned because whilst he had being staying with his dad I noticed cigarette burns on his legs – something I obviously had to report and that will always stay with me. Unfortunately, due to a lack of funding we were never given training to deal with such harrowing issues, we had to develop our own coping mechanisms. I started moving back from the case work soon after that, whilst still liaising with prison officers, lawyers for the families, attending court hearings and making home visits to some families. There were lovely families who would invite me into their homes, however as a volunteer, you have to know your boundaries – not everyone needs or wants your help

RAG became quite a strong force – we lobbied that the government would stop detaining refugees and eventually that stopped. I must say I sometimes saw my role as a volunteer like balancing a delicate knife act at times, on the one hand I was working with the authorities, and on the other hand I was working on behalf of the detainees. You had to be a certain animal, to walk such a fine line – one that I will never forget and neither regret.

RAG remains in operation today and is a coalition of NGOs, voluntary sector organisations, refugees and individuals with an interest in refugee issues in Northern Ireland. The aim of the group is to be an independent voice advocating on asylum and refugee issues, and to be supportive to the refugee and asylum seeking community in Northern Ireland. ,

This picture was drawn by one of the detainees and used by the Refugee Action Group in one of its publications.

Today Crumlin Road Gaol is a major tourist attraction. Promotional material courtesy Belfast City Council

BARNEY McCAUGHEY *Farset International*

'In the early seventies I was employed in the Belfast Office of a national industrial training consultancy. My boss was carrying out a review and planning exercise with the NI Association of Youth Clubs and asked for my thoughts on his design for the weekend consultation conference. I commented on the importance of providing support to ensure the small groups' reports were accurate and well recorded. Naturally I got the job to provide the support – on a voluntary basis!

As a result of this involvement I continued helping the Association's Council work through the review decisions and carry out their implementation. A year or two later I was Chairman and after two years in that role spent three years as Chairman of the Association Training Committee. For me, this was a very creative and satisfying period working with a team of very able people.

Later in the 1970s, the consultancy I worked for recruited a very talented young man who had worked for the Community Relations Commission for some years and was heavily involved in community development initiatives in his personal life.

> *I must admit to finding myself the student, not the teacher on a great many occasions.*

He persuaded us to tender for work with Belfast City Council evaluating larger community groups in Belfast; a new area of work for us. We got the work but couldn't gain access to all the community groups involved. There was resistance to management consultancy coming into the community and voluntary sector – what would they know?

At a European Commission function I accidentally met two men from Woodvale Community and we hit it off until they mentioned the Council Evaluation, their views on it and management consultants generally. I identified myself and my role in the evaluation. We had a very purposeful and heated discussion and departed in disagreement.

A week later one of the men, Jackie Hewitt, who had been leading the opposition, contacted the City Council to demand I start the evaluation

Map of the location of Farset International

Farset Hotel Fashion Show supports children of Chernobyl

ABOVE LEFT: A young model struts her stuff at the Farset Hotel Fashion Show in support of children from Chernobyl. The fashion show was organised by West Belfast charity, the Chernoybl Children's Appeal and leading stores such as ELVI 16+, Liberty Blue and Tesco dontated clothing for the event which was held last Sunday

ABOVE: Young models show off some funky trends from Tesco and Liberty Blue at the Farset Hotel Fashion Show in support of children from Chernobyl

RIGHT: Summer fashions went down a storm at the Farset Hotel Fashion Show organised by West Belfast charity, the Chernoybl Children's Appeal

Article in Andersonstown News, *2nd April 2007*

immediately. I have been working with him ever since.

The Ainsworth Avenue Community Association where Jackie was involved, had a large number of people and they had a whole seething, growing cauldron of ideas, hopes and aspirations. Although the City Council evaluation was completed quickly, I kept going back and over a year later I managed to tease out a second report, a really meaningful articulation of the values, ideas and hopes of all those involved for the future of their community, and with plans to match.

And so Farset Youth and Community Development was born. I agreed to attend the inaugural meeting to chair the elections. Somehow I became the first Chairman, later President, and have been heavily involved ever since.

Although my work led to me spending considerable time outside Ireland and the UK I managed to keep my Farset roles until 1995 when I became self-employed and became even more widely involved, including some years as Chairman of the Greater Shankill Partnership Board.

Whilst I came into the community / voluntary world as an evaluator, using ideas, concepts and experiences from the private and statutory sectors, I must admit to finding myself the student, not the teacher on a great many occasions.

SOPHIE BRYSON *NIACRO*

'BACK IN THE MID seventies when my children were at school, I found I had mornings free. I got involved with different voluntary bodies, for example the Save the Children Play Group. That started my voluntary work.

In the early 1990s I got involved in NIACRO. I had trained as a volunteer at the Citizens Advice Bureau in the 1980s, then I got an ACE post in Prison Link - a joint initiative between NIACRO and the Probation Service.

ACE fizzled out, so I thought, well, I'll just stay on and tie things over in NIACRO: helping families of prisoners with their social security. They would get tangled up in the system and needed help to sort it out.

With NIACRO there is a remarkable wealth of experience brought to the organisation by its volunteers. It had family workers. When people are sent to prison, the prisoner is asked *'can we contact your family about social security?'.* That contact would land on my desk.

I would usually go to the people's homes. Some people might have mental health problems or have families with small children. Some people think everyone is talking about them and they don't want to go out. It gives you that feeling that you can

> *When a family member is sent to prison the family is under so much stress.*

make a difference to someone's life.

I'm quite inquisitive and want to know about people: what can I do to help them and to change their present situation?

Some people can't read the forms or letters, or end up hanging on the phone for ages. I can phone up the social security office on their behalf.

It's just helping someone who's in a fix, and introducing them to some solutions that they wouldn't know about.

When a family member is sent to prison the family is under so much stress. For some their health goes wrong, there are so many complexities. Sometimes you wonder how would you manage if you had all of these disasters? Yet some are so strong.

The stress of a prison sentence on the whole family is so strong. Some mothers might say when a young person is sent to Hydebank – *'At least I know where he is'.* Some family members are very shocked, and just need someone to talk to who is non-judgemental.

When a family member goes into prison, families can grow apart. Quite often the woman becomes stronger and becomes the leader in the family. You can see family dynamics changing. '

GARETH LEE *QueerSpace*

'MY VOLUNTEER STORY INVOLVES my work with QueerSpace over the past ten years. I stumbled across it about a month after it opened. It was like a coffee lounge – I called in with a friend, had a coffee and left. I didn't know what to expect – I thought it'd be like Starbucks.

One weekend I was working and didn't want to go out drinking. Instead I went to QueerSpace at eight or nine in the evening – and there was this drama going on. It was inter-active – they would ask people from the audience to act out the ending. It was a small space so you had to interact. I remember thinking 'How am I going to get out of here?' But I joined in and made contact with people.

There was one woman – Jocelyn – she lived near me, I bumped into her and she encouraged me to go to a meeting the following Wednesday. It was all very causal but interesting – a great mix of people – and I started going to every single meeting since then.

There were opportunities to get involved. I could see that things needed done. I liked the way it was a collective – there was no hierarchy. It was genuinely people working together, all volunteers, with specific roles – from looking after the keys and money, to distributing posters and flyers.

I began to volunteer more time to the project – at that time it was open seven days a week from 10am to 10pm. It was very laid back and easy going – we were making it up as we went along. I met some really interesting people, different ages and backgrounds, different political backgrounds – a lot of my own perceptions were knocked on the head.

It wasn't like work – it was extremely social. Over the years the organisation changed completely. It was evolving, dynamics changed. It depends on the individuals involved – so many people come and go, and bring their skills to the organisation.

queerspace.org.uk

We'd our tenth anniversary celebrations last year – it was amazing the people who came out of the woodwork, who came along and gave their support.

QueerSpace is a safe place and a non-alcoholic space for the LGB community to socialise. We are often marginalised within the community, QueerSpace started before Section 75, there were no civil marriages or protection under the law – there was a need for a vibrant, cultural and social space, without alcohol.

The ethos was a not-for-profit, activist factory. Somewhere to socialise for different reasons – to drop in, but end up getting involved in public consultations, working with other groups – like Pride, and setting up other support groups – like L Plus – for older people. What was happening was evolutionary – that was the beauty of it – we were getting things up and running and off the ground.

People would say – 'QueerSpace – why are you going there – it's all a bunch of lesbians'. I had my perceptions challenged and became a bit of a feminist. I'd get involved in all sorts and take people for who they were. What's kept me involved is the social interaction and that there is no alcohol and it's drug free – that's crucial.

We take the lead, we've built a good reputation and work closely with other groups like CoSo. There are quite a lot of political animals involved in QueerSpace – and we get fully engaged in public consultation and into LGB issues, engaging, working with the Mediation NI people, holding discussions in our own community about gender, race, religion.

Life has certainly changed for the LGBT community in so far as there is legal protection now. Political leadership has been challenged – Cara Friend, CoSo, the Rainbow Project all have staff now. We'd hear stories of people being attacked, assaulted – it still happens.

There are many benefits from being involved in QueerSpace. It enabled me to come out at work. Once a colleague approached me about a year ago – he had started to self harm. We were able to talk openly and honestly and in a constructive way. These are the unexpected benefits.

Volunteering has enabled me to be who I am. It gives you confidence on so many levels, what you put in you get out.

I've been in so many interesting situations – if you'd said to me five or six years ago that I would be giving evidence in front of the Northern Ireland Affairs Committee in the City Hall I would not have believed it, but I was fired up and knew it was important. I'm just an ordinary person, but being part of QueerSpace enabled me to do it.

MICHAEL HALL *Island Pamphlets*

'   I was born in 1949 in East Belfast, close to Harland & Wolff Shipyard. Although I lived within the 'Protestant community', my upbringing was secular and socialist. I participated in the civil rights campaign of 1968-9 and was at Burntollet Bridge when a civil rights march to Derry was attacked by Protestants. Apart from the physical hurts I received, that experience had a profound impact on me, for I realised that my non-sectarian upbringing had not prepared me for the depths of hatred now being unleashed, on both sides, within this society.

Dismayed at the way events were unfolding, I was part of a small group who endeavoured to stimulate a grassroots debate, which we felt was completely lacking. As part of this we produced a booklet which was equally critical of Unionist discrimination and the Provisional IRA's bombing campaign. I was surprised that the document was even read by any of the protagonists but a few weeks after its publication a message was passed through to me, via a friend, from the Provos: 'Tell yer mate that if he writes anything like that again he'll get his knees ventilated.' Shortly afterwards I received an equally blunt threat from Loyalists.

In the mid-1970s, feeling that little of a cross-community nature could be achieved while the extremes were dictating events, my wife and I left Northern Ireland and hitch-hiked around Asia for over a year. When we returned I went to Queen's University and completed a degree in social work. I then joined the NSPCC, where I was allowed to develop my own community-orientated approach to social work. However, when this approach encountered obstacles I resigned and went self-employed as a small publisher.

Around this time I also acted as voluntary co-ordinator of Kinder Community House, a residential centre located in Killough, Co.

Cranes – Harland and Wolff. Photo: Stanley Matchett

Down, funded by the Dutch charity Pax Christi Kinderhulp.

I still retained hopes of encouraging a grassroots debate, especially as the media continued to reinforce stereotypical views of both communities and it was obvious that ordinary people were not being given a proper voice. In May 1988 I attempted to initiate what I termed a 'cross-community think tank' but it met with problems and never got off the ground.

Then, in 1990, I began preparatory work for a series of pamphlets which I hoped would deal with questions of history, culture and politics in a challenging manner.

In December 1991, during a discussion with former Loyalist prisoner Billy Hutchinson – then manager of Springfield Inter-Community Development Project (SICDP) – the idea of establishing 'community think tanks' was resurrected, for it was a concept Billy had also been considering. The first 'think tank' discussions to be set in place were the product of a close collaboration between SICDP and myself, and the pamphlets detailing these discussions were published under my own imprint, Island Publications. The initiative was eventually awarded EU peace funding and launched as Farset Community Think Tanks Project.

Basically, each 'think tank' involves a series of discussions undertaken by a variety of grassroots groups: victims, ex-prisoners, Loyalists, Republicans, young people, senior citizens, community activists… and others. These discussions have been held in different locations: Falls Road, Shankill Road, Short Strand, Ballymacarrett… and as far afield as Strabane and Derry. Each participating group determines its own agenda and is in full control of the process. My role, apart from facilitating and recording the discussions, is to edit – but not censor – the transcripts into a readable and accessible pamphlet. The initial funding allowed for 2000 copies of each pamphlet to be widely disseminated, free of charge, around the community network. To date, over 180,000 pamphlets have been distributed.

From the project's inception community groups began to see a value in not only exploring issues pertinent to their own community, but in using the think tank process as a means of engaging purposefully across 'the divide'. Some very challenging discussions have addressed highly controversial issues, such as marching and parades, and often these discussions have involved participants from both communities. One academic commented that the pamphlet series represents a unique record of a society in transition. Indeed, the 93 pamphlets published to date contain within them over 1,250,000 words of oral testimony. A full list of the pamphlets can be found at http://cain.ulst.ac.uk/islandpublications/ – some two dozen titles can be downloaded free.

As well as being available in numerous community venues the pamphlets have been displayed in places as diverse as the Green Cross Art and Book Shop (which adjoins the Sinn Féin advice centre on the Falls Road) and shops selling Loyalist merchandise on the Shankill and Newtownards Roads. Despite the fact that some pamphlets have been very critical of Republicanism, while others have been equally critical of Loyalism, these outlets were more than willing to display all the titles, because the purpose behind the pamphlet series, that of encouraging and facilitating debate and dialogue, was readily accepted by both sides. As for downtown bookshops, to my disappointment Waterstones and Easons declined to stock the pamphlets; only the Bookshop at Queens and the Linen Hall Library proved supportive.

The think tanks and pamphlets have also helped to extend the parameters of grassroots debate. For example, the second series of discussions undertaken by the Shankill Think Tank produced some very progressive thinking, and the participants had a concern that the views expressed might be running too far ahead of local attitudes. However, Shankill Road community worker May Blood later told me that she had attended a community meeting where she was pleased, and surprised, that formerly taboo topics were being addressed. When she asked how this had come about she was told: 'Well, if the Shankill Think Tank can discuss such things, then so can we.'

Another participant described the experience of being involved in a think tank discussion as 'therapeutic' – because for the first time she had been allowed to express her views openly, and her personal story had been accorded an equal value.

The Troubles have left an appalling legacy of hurt and trauma. Only by allowing that legacy to be addressed – and expressed – freely, honestly and without manipulation can we hope to move forward into a more equal and pluralist society. Additionally, only through genuine debate and dialogue will we be able to put aside old fears and prejudices and work constructively to build a more tolerant society for future generations.

ANNE COLLINS *Shopmobility*

'It all started when I became the Secretary of the Disabled Drivers Association in 1994.

I got polio when I was six and a half. I'd been involved with the Disabled Drivers Association since I was sixteen as a volunteer, usually writing endless letters.

In the 1980s pedestrianism came in all over the place – it was the new buzzword. We knew it was only a matter of time before it arrived in Belfast, and we knew how much it would affect disabled drivers.

I first heard about Shopmobility when I was at a Disabled Drivers conference in the Midlands (of England). There were delegates from all over Northern Ireland and we thought it was a great idea. There were already sixty to seventy Shopmobility schemes in GB. The first one was started in Milton Keynes which was the first major town to be pedestrianised. Shopmobility just seemed to grow from that.

Shopmobility started in Belfast in 1998 – it took two years to get off the ground. We went out and talked to anyone and everyone about it .

We squatted in a unit at the Victoria Centre. We officially opened on 4th December 1997, and the Lord Mayor did the opening. We were going to open the week before but Clinton was here on his second visit.

It was very exciting. I worked as a volunteer to keep it all going. Belfast City Council paid for the insurance. There were stumbling blocks along the way, many regulations – a lot of people said it couldn't happen in Northern Ireland.

In the first year it was entirely run by volunteers, and we still have some of those same volunteers with us ten to twelve years on.

VOLUNTEER
OPPORTUNITIES

Shopmobility *Getting you around* Belfast

They were incredible. Say for example we said we needed a vacuum, then one would appear; if someone said they needed a stapler, someone else would say they had a spare one at home and bring it in. Post Office Counters donated all the furniture. One day the DoE had an auction and I went along with £20 and bought two glass fronted bookcases and a board table – we still use these today.

At first it was very hard persuading the volunteers to use the scooters. I was familiar with my scooter and knew the freedom it gave me around the house. They were soon persuaded.

We got a grant from Making Belfast Work and Belfast Action Team. It meant we could now employ a member of staff and an advertisement for the post went into the press.

Nothing was further from the truth than the thought that I should apply for the post. But Peter McLachlan asked me if I was ready to step back and let someone else take over my baby, and so at the eleventh hour, I put in my application, and was offered the post.

For the first six months I was on trial, and I was sailing on the seat of my pants. Peter McLachlan tried to tie me down with

> *At first it was very hard persuading the volunteers to use the scooters.*

procedures – Peter and I had many a barney, but he was right and I was wrong.

Peter was setting up functions for the organisation that we were to become and that we are today and will be in twenty years time. He made me do things like write job descriptions, a staff handbook, and so on. We are reaping the rewards now of the labours we did then.

We relied and rely on volunteers – I was the only paid member of staff, and after a while I got an assistant. Shopmobility could not function without its volunteers. They form the core of this organisation.

When I think back they were very exciting times - great times. We had so many ideas and suggestions. It was a bit like Blue Peter - it was sellotape and scissor time, and we didn't know what would happen next.

At times it was frightening – Shopmobility had happened in England but a lot of people said it wouldn't happen here but it did. At first we had to get the volunteers to take the scooters out and about to make it look good and the volunteers did the same. We gave leaflets out to anyone who looked like they might have a mobility difficulty, and asked them politely – '*why don't you try it*'? And it just grew and grew. It was a very good approach and very powerful.

The powerbase just seemed to happen. People used the equipment, and then we asked people if they would like to come in and volunteer. It was like they had been waiting for you to say it. They loved it and were pleased to be asked.

We have volunteers who do everything. I am always surprised by our volunteers. They will say 'I know someone who will come in and do that', and they do.

VINCENT BENT *Quaker Service*

'I've been with the Quaker Service committee since March 1980. Part of getting to know the organisation was to go to the Maze to familiarise myself with the work that was done there.

Monica Barritt ran the centre as a volunteer. She made sure all the volunteers were in place herself. There was a part time driver who did prison runs for outlying places where there was no public transport.

There was tremendous spirit among the volunteers. People came to the centre from right across the board, from all over Northern Ireland. Politics and religion were left aside.

The volunteers were there to assist the families. My impression was that prisoners' families were not high on most people's agendas.

The Society of Friends realised that whatever the men had done – whether they should or shouldn't be there – their families and their children were usually unaware of that and were completely innocent.

The centre was a temporary building provided by the prison. It was very limited. Most people coming to the centre were women. The volunteers played a valuable role in giving in the most simple sense – just a cup of tea and a snack. They were there to show that someone cared. These women were very loyal to their husbands. They made the terrible journey – some from very far away – to maintain family links. For some this was very hard to do. They would look their best and put on a brave front. They gave the impression that everything was okay. At times they needed someone to talk to if it was a bad visit. Sometimes they would come out and break down in tears. Monica Barritt or one of the volunteers would take them into the office quietly, for a cup of tea and a listening ear. It was not counselling, just a non-threatening listening ear. She could tell her story, and share the difficulties of what she was going through to someone who was non-judgemental.

The prisoner centre had been set up in 1971 so by 1980 it had been running for eight or nine years. It was simple fare – homemade soup, sausage rolls, crackers and biscuits. The sustenance was

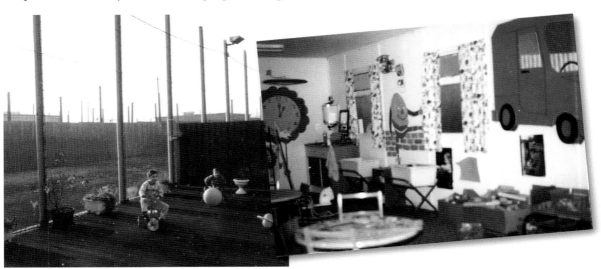

Maze Visitor Centre. Photos Quaker service

important – but for me, the most important thing was the manner in which it was served. Sometimes people didn't want to talk. They were treated with dignity and respect. The volunteers would not have condoned what the men had done, but they got to know the women who came week in and week out.

The volunteers had empathy with the women. The key thing for me was the atmosphere. It was an oasis of calm in that no-one talked about the situation. When they stepped through the door they left their affiliation behind. At certain times the canteen would be full – people from the nationalist/Catholic tradition in the same room with people from the Protestant/loyalist tradition. They accepted their differences – they were all in the same boat.

Even during the Hunger Strikes and around difficult times – for example the breakout when a prison officer was shot dead, the centre retained a degree of calm.

Many volunteers – women from the older generation, who had ceased work but had seen a lot of life; housewives who had raised their own children – some would work once a week, or once a month. There was a rota system and the volunteers were very loyal. They came when they said they would. Monica ran it very smoothly and the volunteers were very co-operative, although I'm sure at times it was difficult. '

ANON *Maze Prison Visitors Centre*

' I became a volunteer on the spur of the moment. I was a nurse at the cancer unit at Belvoir. My matron was a volunteer at the Maze prison and she asked would I be a volunteer – so we went together.

It must have around '75 or '76. It was the height of the troubles but there were good volunteers at the prison – good workers, a cross section of people. I wanted to do as much as I could.

I remember the mothers coming to visit their sons – that's what stood out for me. They looked so worried, grey haired. There would be young children coming and going in mini-bus loads.

People would be coming in a state, children would be running wild, grandmothers would be visiting with their families, always in an anxious state – but they were supported in a nice way – they were made to feel comfortable. You just went and did your bit, you didn't ask questions. There were 3000 prisoners at the height of the troubles.

To be a volunteer there meant you didn't get a minute – making sandwiches, washing plates, pans,

preparing vegetables, cleaning veg, serving behind the counter – saying, here, have a seat, a cup of tea, a sandwich, a breather.

Some would be disappointed, and would have to wait a lot of weeks to get another visit. They would be standing thick like sardines – they were coming from all over Ulster, and sometimes they were just glad to be looked after.

My memory of the Maze – what stands out – is the old grey haired women, how unhappy looking they were. '

MRS KHAN *Al-Nisa Association*

'I came to Belfast in 1986 from Karachi in Pakistan. I'd been working in Saudi Arabia as a ward sister and as a deputy matron in Pakistan. I came to join my husband who was already here – he is a Consultant Cardiologist at the RVH.

Since I came here I didn't work – or rather I didn't work as a paid worker – but have been doing voluntary work, and looking after my husband and my family. I felt there was a need for Muslim women to get together – there was a sense of isolation. I didn't have my mother, sister, brother. I had three sons. A lot of Muslin women were at home, yet in any new country you need to know a number of things, to share feelings with women – there are some things that are easier to share than with men.

At the Belfast Islamic Centre in Wellington Park there was a community centre. I started a women's group and we began by meeting there and discussing social things, and chatted about how to support each other.

I was selected to represent women on the Executive Committee of the Belfast Islamic Centre. This was a positive step – a chance to start something new, but it took time and courage convincing people.

In 1998 we became a totally independent organisation, with our own elections and committee. We started dealing with our own affairs. When we were still in the Islamic Centre, Section 75 legislation was introduced. We published the first edition of the Muslim Culture and Traditions Information Pack to provide information about Islamic customs and practices to health, social services, the police and other agencies.

Al-Nisa (The Women) has opened doors for me. I was on the Board of Directors for the Multi Cultural Resource Centre and the Board of the Northern Ireland Council for Ethnic Minorities. We were working together with an all-party group of political leaders. Ethnic minority groups worked with government departments on the implementation of the OFMDFM Race Equality Strategy.

In 2001 we moved out of the Belfast Islamic centre. We had no funding and no premises. At first Women's Aid supplied us with some space in South Belfast.

We believe that the work should be done by volunteers. We can be contacted at any time. We also provide an interpreting and translating service.

Volunteers find it hard to give one hundred per cent of their time. Some women have jobs, are involved in businesses, or have small children.

We are now compiling existing translations of the Qur'an in three different languages (English, Urdu and Arabic). It will take a long time. All this work is being done by volunteers, and in the meantime, the 24 hour help line continues, the website continues, our sign-posting services continue.'

Wom

To Roman

Emma Ringland is a yo
inspiration to all. **Jenny Lee**
of Romania and th

EMMA RINGLAND'S passion and love for the people of Romania is so obvious to all who know her.

Bubbly and enthusiastic, Emma's eyes light up the moment she starts to talk about the children and people who clearly melted her heart.

Modest Emma (24), from Crossgar, is just one of many unsung heroes from Northern Ireland who give up there time to help others.

Over the past three years Emma has visited Romania on a number of occasions, to work with and show love to disadvantaged children and adults in orphanages, refuges and Aids hospitals.

Emma first got involved with volunteer work during a year-out after university when she was accepted for a years placement with Voluntary Service Belfast in their Young Citizens in Action programme.

This involved working for the VSB youth office as well as a community placement working with young offenders and befriending a girl with special support needs for a year.

"I have always wanted to work with children and in the field of social work. I had the qualifications but I needed more experience to get a job," she said.

VSB offer volunteer opportunities for all aged 16 and up, at a time, place and pace which suits the individual.

"During my time at VSB I also completed RSA training in youth work and a certificate in counselling. It was the best decision ever and prepared me for going on to work."

Emma started work in Thorndale family assessment centre in Belfast in October 2000 as a family support worker, but the summer before this she got her first experience of Romania, travelling with a team of 25 from VSB.

"It was something I always wanted to do from a young age when I saw the horrific images on television and was moved at the plight of the children.

"When I knew there was an opportunity for me to go, I was in and once there I knew it wouldn't be my last visit.

"There is something magical about Romania – it just brings you back everytime."

On her first visit and after a three hour drive on bumpy roads from Bucharest to Brasov, Emma was shocked that it looked better than she imagined.

"I first saw the city centre of Brasov and it was really well off. Beautiful buildings and gorgeous scenery.

"But, as you go further and further into the country its gets poorer and poorer and the whole appearance changes from modern building to really old prehistoric living."

It is 10 years since pictures of Romanian orphanages first flooded our television screens. Whilst the images are not as horrific as we first encountered, there is still much need. The economic conditions in Romania are not improving and most people find it ever more difficult to survive.

The city of Brasov that Emma visited is about the size of Belfast and is in a province the size of Northern Ireland.

One of the most sickening images Emma encountered was of young children tied to cots in an orphanage for kids with learning disabilities, to prevent them from harming themselves.

"The conditions were terrible. I've never saw kids as pleased to see water."

Emma explained to me that bottled water was a special treat for the children as they are normally not allowed to drink as it only causes them to wet themselves which is an inconvenience for the carers, giving them extra work.

"Just stopping for a minute and stroking a child's face stops them hitting themselves. They look at you and smile. It takes no effort to do that, but the workers don't care."

Another sad sight Emma saw was donated toys locked away in cupboards.

"Everything is on show, teddy bears are even pinned on walls – when we take them down and hand them to a child it makes their day," she said.

Emma was also involved in practical work, such as painting colourful path stones and building a playground.

The plight of orphanages is synonymous in Romania, but there is also the forgotten elderly who only receive £4 benefits each month.

"We also helped out at a refuge for 100 older people with mental health problems and brought them blankets," said Emma.

"The refuge was an old delapidated building, where we found beds with four frail people huddled up together for heat."

However things are looking more hopeful in Romania as a whole, thanks mainly to the aid and assistance from people with a big heart like Emma, who each time she visits does see some improvements.

"Thankfully the refuge is becoming more and more like a hospital and the patients are getting treatment and therapy."

Northern Ireland young people who go to Romania make a difference, not only through the aid they bring and the work they do, but also the longer lasting impact they make through building up relationships.

Last summer the YCIN team saved a Juvenile Centre, where street children lifted by the authorities and children in care are sent, from being closed down by renewing its plumbing system.

The team impacted upon these childrens lives by playing with them, taking them on trips and holding discos.

"The kids keep in touch through their teacher, who sends me letters from time to time, saying things like 'I miss you' to 'You are my sister'".

Emma particularly stays in touch with Romina, now

> **Just stopping for a minute and stroking a child's face stops them hitting themselves. They look at you smile. It takes no effort to do that, but the workers don't care**

Emma Ringland

Article from The Irish News, 3 April 2002

nen Talk

nia with love...

ung woman with a heart of gold and an
speaks to her about her love for the people
e volunteer work she is involved in

■ **LOCAL HERO:** Emma Ringland makes friends wherever she goes in Romania and her volunteer work has helped many children have a better start in life

18-years old, even phoning her from time to time.
"It is great to witness the changes in Romina's life and see the opportunities she is now getting. The centre have sent her to a computer course and her dream is to come over here to work – I'm half expecting her to arrive on my doorstep anytime.
"It is very sad though that when the teenagers reach a certain age they are likely to be put back onto the streets again. Romina is lucky, it is a vicious circle.
"This summer I will be working with the street kids, it's just another world and heartbreaking to see kids sleeping in sewers," said Emma.
To volunteer in Romania, members of the team are asked to fundraise at least $600 each. Emma far exceeds this amount each time and is extremely grateful to the support she has received. She especially says a big thank you to her mother and the community of Comber who support her famous coffee mornings.
"The generosity is so amazing, that is why they turn out so successful," said Emma.
Emma also holds car boot sales, raffles and theme nights. She will also embark upon a sponsored abseil down BT tower on May 11.

"We can bring out as much money as they want, but more important is working with the kids. That is priceless. Stimulating, interacting and communicating with them mean more than anything."
Emma has continued her volunteer work in Romania under the banner of Inter Aid, a registered charity co-ordinated by Northern Ireland men Richard Holmes and Ernest Crawford.
Emma's last visit to Romania was just before Christmas, which was an entirely different experience.
As well as stalking up stores with food for the winter time, she also spent time sleighing in the snow with the children.
"It is the best experience ever to see smiling children coming running towards you for a hug. It is so brilliant now when they remember my name."
Emma, who hopes to undertake a social work diploma, doesn't rule out the possibility of maybe working out in Romania full-time some day.
In the Brasov region, there are four social workers with a case load of 600 families each.
"They do an amazing job, but there needs to be much more resources available to them," she said.

Emma can't wait to go out to Romania again later this month, to sort out arrangements for the Inter Aid team visit in June/July.
"I will be meeting the directors at the orphanages, finding out about our new projects and see what is needed."
There are hundreds of ways you can volunteer both in your community and overseas. Why not take Emma's example and give a little back and bring a smile to someone's face?
Volunteering with Inter Aid offers you a challenge, personal development and the opportunity to improve the lives of kids and adults in Romania.
If anyone is interested in getting involved with Inter Aid or helping Emma financially through sponsorship, by donating prizes for raffles, you can email **emmaringland@hotmail.com** or contact Jenny Lee at *the Irish News.*

IF you have an interesting or inspirational story that you would like to share then please send a brief outline (less than 100 words) to Joanna Braniff (features editor) 113-117 Donegall Street, Belfast, BT1 2GE or email it to j.braniff@irish-news.com. We look forward to hearing from you.

PETER EMERSON *de Borda Institute*

Political Awarness Pack produced by young people

After leaving school with an 'A' level or few, I became a Naval Officer in submarines, and initially thought that would be my career. Yet I had a funny feeling from day one that this might be just a temporary sojourn. Later on, having seen a lot of poverty in the third world, I decided to opt out. I knew I was not part of the solution to this question. I didn't realise then that I was actually part of the problem. It took four years to get out.

I then went to VSO, to see what use retired naval officers could be to the third world. Not much they said. But I went anyway, and became a teacher of maths and physics in Starehe, a school for the poor in Nairobi. I was also a house master and sports master. And every holidays, a colleague and I – he was from VSO – took groups of boys to climb the mountains of East Africa – it is an incredible part of the world.

I stayed there for three and a half years, and then, in 1974, I cycled for over 10,000 kilometres across Central Africa on a push-bike, from Nairobi, via Kinshasa, to Lagos and Lusaka, and back to Nairobi. It took me eight wonderful, exciting months.

I also went to India, to work in Mother Teresa's hospital for the dying in Calcutta. And then I came home, travelling over land, now by bus and train. Why people like flying, I have no idea!

In July 1974 I got a letter from VSB – I was half

way round Africa, poste restante in Zaire. Hang on, I said. And I came to Belfast six months later, in January '75, and volunteered for Cairn Lodge Boys' Club on the Crumlin Road. So the first thing to do was to let the girls in to what then became Cairn Lodge Youth Club. Despite being a Catholic working in a Protestant area, I was ok, for with my English accent they all assumed I was a Protestant. Initially anyway. It meant I could start some cross-community work, mixing with some neighbouring youth clubs, in Ardoyne.

In 1977, having just resigned on a matter of principle from my job as a community worker in Ardoyne, I was unemployed. Aware of my plight, a friend showed me a derelict old gate lodge on the Ballysillan Road, so I squatted – Rhubarb Cottage. So now I had all the time to do the things that I really wanted to do, campaigning for, well, a better world. I had to sort out the house, of course, to legitimise my tenancy, and then my ownership. It had been empty for some time, and I didn't know who owned it. But once I'd lived there for twelve years, uncontested, I had squatter's rights. It gave me the freedom to be political, and I became 'green' in a political sense. I still had my bicycle, and now I'd got a bit of land as well. My garden now boasts an olive tree, a kiwi, and a magnificent vine – all signs of global warming, but all potentially, and some already, delicious.

I had joined the Liberal Party, and the Liberal Ecology Group. But the Liberal Party was not really concerned about what was going on over here, and I was virtually the only person in Belfast attending the annual Liberal conferences. At one of these, someone said why don't you set up a Northern Ireland CND. It soon became a full time unpaid occupation – I was a volunteer in the full sense of the word – at the peace camp at RAF Bishopscourt.

By this time I was involved in civil disobedience, very much on the Ghandian model of pacifism, which seemed even more appropriate in the Troubles of Northern Ireland. We fasted, in good

Peter Emerson with bike outside Rhubarb Cottage

humour and with self sacrifice. There was one seven day salt and water fast, and we also broke in to the government nuclear bunker off the Malone Road .

I had already done a fast in 1978 outside Stormont. That was because of the shenanigans in Westminster, when Callaghan – it was the last days of his government – went into power with the Unionists, giving them more seats in Westminster, but without introducing PR. It was January, and it was cold – I was there day and night – but if you're into the philosophy of self sacrifice, that's what you do...

I joined the Green Party in 1982, and was there at the founding convention, in Glencree. Before we could launch a branch up here, however, we had to have a specific policy on the Northern Ireland question. It took us a year, and then, in May 1983, at a press conference in the Europa, with fellow Greens from across the water and the border, the NI Green Ecology Party was duly launched.

But I digress. Crossing peace lines. CND. And to live without being fluent in at least one other language was not good – so in 1983, I started to learn Russian. I was forty years old. One year later, I became a mature student in Russian studies, at Queen's University.

In 1985 a few of us held yet another pacifist demonstration. It was the time of the Anglo-Irish agreement and Paisley was marching around throughout Northern Ireland with his tens of thousands. So six of us stood, outside the City Hall, with a huge banner which read: "We have to say yes to something". It was, if you like, a constructive vote of no confidence. If you don't like something, you should come up with some other solution and stop being a spoilt child, constantly saying 'no'!

Next, I organised a conference for the New Ireland Group – where we were going to use concensus voting rather than majority vote. Indeed, the conference was novel in many respects: we sat in a circle, sat in silence as if we were Quakers, and listened to a poem which the late John Hewitt had written especially for the occasion. Sinn Féin, Unionist, the political wing of the UDA, not the DUP – we did try to get them there, and even Ulster Clubs – 250 people were there and it was brilliant. Furthermore, with consensus voting, we identified their common consensus: 'Northern Ireland to have power sharing under a Tripartite Belfast-London-Dublin agreement'. It was a mini Good Friday Agreement, if you like, just twelve years ahead of its time.

We held a few more of these consensus gatherings, but then I got a grant to study Russian in Moscow. And in 1988, I started work as a translator there. I went to Russia on a bike, across Poland; and in 1990, I came home by bike, via the Balkans.

I organised another conference for the Northern Ireland Group, now with electronic computer voting. There was an even greater cross-section of attendees, with one MEP and two TDs, not to mention future MLAs. And again, it worked:

we found their consensus. But yet, in the Belfast Talks which followed, not one participant, not one academic, and not one journalist even mentioned consensus voting.

So, in 1998, a few friends and I decided to set up the de Borda Institute. Both before and since, we have done quite a bit of work – going to conflict zones in the Balkans and the Caucasus: before, to warn of the dangers; during, to report; and after the conflicts, to try and help heal the wounds. We have written articles, conducted interviews, given lectures, published books, and developed our own computer soft-ware; and partly because I also speak some Serbo-Croat – it's very similar to Russian – I have often worked for the OSCE (Organisation for Security and Co-operation in Europe) as an election observer, throughout Central and Eastern Europe. In addition, I have taught consensus politics in East and Southern Africa .

But talking of elections, I have also stood for the Green Party in pretty well every local and Assembly election in Oldpark and North Belfast, not only in my own time but, at least initially, at my own expense. Indeed, standing in 1981, three of us were the first on this island to stand under the 'ecology' label, but the press didn't know what that word meant, so a few years later, throughout these islands, we all called ourselves the Green Party.

Most recently, after the 2008 conflict in South Ossetia, I was working for Irish Aid as a Russian/ English interpreter in Georgia. And I have just returned from a lecture tour of the United States, where the de Borda Institute now has a more international profile.

I've done what I've done because I enjoy it. If you don't enjoy it you won't be good at it. I've also done what I've done because I felt it was what I should be doing. I have very few regrets.

THE
AGREEMENT

**THIS AGREEMENT IS ABOUT <u>YOUR</u> FUTURE.
PLEASE READ IT CAREFULLY.**

It's Your Decision

PEOPLE AND PLACE

AT ONE TIME
A personal reflection by Sir Kenneth Bloomfield

I am, unfortunately, old enough to recall how people responded to the challenge posed by the Second World War. I remember, as a small boy, accompanying my mother on occasions to the ARP post at Ballyhackamore, where she manned one of the telephones to receive messages about possible air attack. In the face of such a crisis, it was taken for granted that citizens would volunteer in different capacities to serve on the "home front". That crisis, with the prospect of invasion and enslavement, was all too obvious. Yet other crises persisted long after the cessation of hostilities; crises of poverty, disadvantage, discrimination and unacceptable living conditions, to name but a few.

In my adult life I would serve for almost forty years in the Northern Ireland Civil Service. Looking back on it now, I feel that for too long the Service saw itself as the sun of a planetary system, with other public services revolving around it as minor planets, and minimal consciousness of the potential of a "third force" of voluntary action. These attitudes were to change substantially, albeit gradually, through the pressure of events and the influence of personalities.

One of my colleagues most conscious of the potential of voluntary effort was Ronnie Spence. I recall vividly the day he came to talk to me, when I was Permanent Secretary at the DOE, about the potential of Housing Associations as a " third force" in tackling the huge problem of replacing those unfit dwellings in which all too many of our people still lived. This model had already been introduced in England, and Ronnie persuaded me that we should follow suit. Thereafter we found ourselves dealing with a diverse range of such Associations, some of them operating in specialist areas of the housing market and drawing on relevant knowledge and expertise, while others had been formed within local communities with abundant ambition by volunteers who did not always have access to business skills and experience. In this specific area, I believe an invaluable contribution was made by the Northern Ireland Federation and such people as Erskine

Holmes, in advising organisations full of enthusiasm but new to the challenge about rules and procedures and the need for accountability.

This supportive role, not pushing local enthusiasm aside but seeking to harness, advise and support it, has been of crucial importance across the whole voluntary sector. NICVA and VSB and other supportive organisations like Bryson House, have helped to realise the huge potential of that sector.

I will refer in a moment to the impact of our euphemistically termed "troubles". We have, though, to remember that there are and have been many other "troubled" communities, even in the developed world. I vividly recall, for example, accompanying the direct rule Environment Minister of the day, Ray Carter, on a visit to the Bedford/Stuyvesant Foundation in New York. There the prevalence of crack cocaine was a warning of a tide of addiction heading our way. Yet, in these most unpromising of circumstances, the local black leadership had thrown up some inspiring figures, who sought to turn back the current of apathy and despair. I remember in particular a charismatic lady of West Indian origin who used a passion for dance to engage the interest of local girls otherwise all too likely to submit to malign influences. What I found particularly interesting was that, while the visible face of the Foundation remained wholly local, there existed in the background a discreet group of " friends" from the prosperous business and professional community in Manhattan, who were able to offer expertise, advice and invaluable contacts not available to the local leadership.

I might add that, although we can be justifiably critical of many aspects of American life, there is a remarkable tradition of people who have achieved great success and prosperity accepting a moral obligation to put something back into the wider society. It seems to me that, by and large, they have given a positive response to the challenging

> *One had to learn how to fill in "the right boxes".*

question, "Pro tanto quid retribuamus?". Our own best and oldest American friends, made in New York almost fifty years ago, have since prospered greatly in the stimulating environment of bustling Chicago. Having achieved this success and attendant prosperity, Mike has focussed all his energy, experience and influence on efforts to improve the public (in the American sense) school system of Chicago, with its majority of black pupils. His Golden Apple Foundation has launched multiple initiatives to improve conditions, boost the morale of the teaching profession and celebrate and reward excellence.

To return, though, to the local scene, the "troubles" presented communities across Northern Ireland with challenges of a unique kind. In many areas there was a growing sense that the public sector alone was incapable to do enough, or to do it quickly enough, to cope with multiple deprivation. A new spirit of self-reliance became increasingly evident. Of course, enthusiasm alone was not enough. There was a need for resources, which could only come from central or local government, from European funding or from other funding bodies such as the great charitable foundations, the Ireland Funds or the International Fund for Ireland. Community leaders had to learn very quickly the black arts of "applicationship", (which should, perhaps, be offered these days as a degree course!). One had to learn how to fill in "the right boxes". As one of those who negotiated with the Americans what would become the International Fund for Ireland it was made clear to me that Congress and the Administration expected the emphasis to be on schemes of economic utility offering long-term benefit rather than on social programmes. It took time for applicants to realise that "Brownie points" were to be won by stressing the employment consequences of social schemes.

Three developments, one occurring before and two after my retirement from the Civil Service, brought me close to some of the animators of the voluntary movement. It may be recalled that it was the young Labour minister, Lord (call me "Peter") Melchett who first focussed on the problems of the so-called "Belfast areas of need". A great deal of effort, and very substantial funding, had been directed to social conditions, with a keynote programme being the investment in a system of modern leisure centres. Unfortunately insufficient account was taken of the long-term revenue costs, which could only be met by rising ratepayer subsidies or the setting of charges at levels beyond the means of those who were supposed to benefit.

By the late Eighties, when I had become Head of the Civil Service, it was all too evident that we needed a "new look" at these problems of multiple deprivation. Richard Needham as minister, harnessing the energies of Forward-looking officials like Ronnie Spence and Nigel Hamilton, launched the programme called " Making Belfast Work", which I then made my top priority in the final years of my bureaucratic career. From the outset Needham saw the need to draw upon the experience, knowledge and enthusiasm of people already working in and for disadvantaged communities, and I remember being greatly impressed by my first contacts with Paul Sweeney, now himself a Permanent Secretary in the Northern Ireland administration.

I was sad to think that these productive and informative contacts with the voluntary sector would come to an end after I left Stormont in 1991. Yet events moved, as they so often do, in unanticipated directions. Joining the Board of the BBC as National Governor for Northern Ireland in 1991, I was asked in the following year to become chairman of the Children in Need Trust, the Corporation's own charitable vehicle. My service in that post for some six

> *The voluntary commitment of individual people to wider communal ends ought to be a touchstone of our values.*

years was a revelation to me. The plight of so many children in Africa and Asia and Latin America was so evident as to turn the gaze of charitable funders elsewhere. Yet I soon came to appreciate how many children still needed help and support in our own communities. I was not surprised to find that Northern Ireland viewers and listeners were amongst the most generous donors, but delighted to learn that , year after year, we here were net beneficiaries from the activities of the Trust. At the London meetings of the trustees, our concern was mostly with broad policy, but here in Northern Ireland I was able to get much closer to the recipients of our support, who were very often modest organisations relying heavily on the work of highly motivated volunteers. At the Northern Ireland end, the distribution of our local "share" rested with the local Appeals Advisory Committee, chaired by another current Permanent Secretary in Aideen McGinley and splendidly served by the remarkable Sheila-Jane Malley, daughter of a close colleague at Stormont Castle during the O'Neill years of the early Sixties. Their preference and policy was to make a large number of comparatively modest grants rather than a much smaller number of big ones. Other potential funders knew that any project funded by Children in Need had been most carefully vetted, and that they could with confidence come alongside the Trust in the support of such a project. On various occasions I would have the satisfaction of handing over cheques to successful applicants. It was very different from my experience in government. In that context the recipient of £10 millions might well complain that it had not been £15 millions. Here, groups receiving £1,000 would be really grateful for it, and I became aware that on occasions quite modest sums of money could result in considerable leverage.

Another informative experience began with Mo Mowlam's invitation to me in 1997 to bring forward

The aftermath of the Remembrance Day bombing in Enniskillen. Photo: Stanley Matchett.

recommendations on how the suffering of victims of the troubles might best be recognised, and although I reported the following year I have in fact been involved in one aspect or another of this issue for more than ten years. I was asked to lead a team to pursue my own recommendation that the system of criminal injuries compensation should be reviewed, and thereafter appointed as the UK Commissioner for the Location of Victims' Remains, a post in which I continue to serve until this day. All these experiences brought me into contact with a range of supportive organisations such as WAVE.

But I am part of a partnership rather than a single individual, and much of my knowledge of the extent and value to society of voluntary effort comes from

The Ian Gow Memorial Fund
FOR YOUNG PEOPLE FROM NORTHERN IRELAND

Final Reflections

Ian Gow was for 16 years MP for Eastbourne; he was Parliamentary Private Secretary to Prime Minister Margaret Thatcher, Minister for Housing and Construction, and Minister of State at the Treasury. On the 30th July 1990, as a result of a provisional IRA bomb he became a victim of the Northern Ireland Troubles.

Members of the Ian Gow Memorial Fund NI Advisory Committee meeting with Dame Jane Gow

In "We Will Remember Them – Report of the Northern Ireland Victims Commissioner", Sir Kenneth Bloomfield described his task as Victims Commissioner as 'a painful privilege: painful because I encountered grief and human suffering on an enormous scale: a privilege, because I encountered such courage, such endurance and – often from those most gravely affected – such generosity of spirit'.

The Gow family extended such "generosity of spirit" in 1990 when, along with friends of Ian, they created a Charitable Trust Fund for the benefit of young people from Northern Ireland. Since 1990 the Ian Gow Memorial Fund has made almost 2,500 individual awards, disbursed in excess of £850,000 and assisted Schools, Universities and Community Groups. In 2001 after ten years the Trustees, the NI Committee and the Gow family felt that it was time to consider bringing the Fund to a close. So, in 2003 the Fund made its final awards to young people and community groups.

It has been a great honour for Voluntary Service Bureau to be associated with the Ian Gow Memorial Fund as it attempted to make a difference to the lives of young people in Northern Ireland. Volunteering is central to Voluntary Service Bureau and it was a privilege therefore to offer administrative support to a lively, enthusiastic and dedicated group of volunteers on the Northern Ireland Advisory Committee.

The policy of the Trustees was to give priority to the support of individual young people through small grants which could make a significant difference to the lives of those suffering from some degree of personal disadvantage. Some grants could be financial assistance to enable a young person to continue with their education, some grants would be for travel, and others to encourage the development of musical talent – in this reflecting a passion of Dame Jane, herself a talented pianist.

Processing and assessing the applications provided a unique insight into the difficulties, hardships and turmoil that many young people in Northern Ireland face as part of their daily existence. The local Committee, whilst at times emotionally overwhelmed with the cases presented by the young people, were equally amazed at their resilience, optimism, talent, commitment to others and sheer joy for life.

The Fund has made an important contribution to the development of many young people from Northern Ireland, helping them to overcome disadvantage and difficulties, achieve personal goals and ambitions, and to improve their future prospects. The Fund as a significant resource will be missed by the young people in Northern Ireland.

Ian Gow Memorial Fund Awards made to Individuals 1991-2003

Year	No. of awards made	Total £
1991	125	35,140
1992	228	49,314
1993	158	22,065
1994	206	38,744
1995	171	32,480
1996	183	35,465
1997	238	55,940
1998	202	41,855
1999	249	43,960
2000	237	52,985
2001	206	39,220
2002	192	36,134
2003	74	22,625
TOTAL:	**2,469**	**£505,927**

Of the awards made to individuals noted above:

- 132 awards were made to 'Victims' of the 'Troubles'
- 83 awards were made to 'Young people with a Disability'
- 36 awards were made to 'Young Offenders'
- 620 'Travel' awards were made to young people covering a diverse range of activities from outward bound courses to Scotland, to expeditions to Mongolia to undertake voluntary work.
- 44 major music awards supported by the Headley Charitable Trust

Additional awards were made by the Trust to Universities, Schools and Community Groups (see overleaf). These awards include donations to Hazelwood College in order to install the 'Ian Gow Memorial Fund Library'.

my wife, Elizabeth, who was free after my retirement to pursue numerous activities of her own, almost all of them designed to promote social action by private sector and voluntary bodies. I would mention three of these in particular, although there have been many more.

After the awful events of Remembrance Day in Enniskillen. Brian Mawhinney played the leading role in establishing the Spirit of Enniskillen Bursaries. He invited Elizabeth to be one of the members of its first board, alongside the late Gordon Wilson and others, and for many years thereafter she took part in interviews with young people seeking the support of this organisation.

Then, as will be recalled, Ian Gow MP became another of the casualties of our prolonged conflict. When those who had admired him and wished to honour his memory considered how best to use the very substantial sums raised for that purpose, they decided to use the funds for the support of young people in Northern Ireland, either as individuals or through their schools. Far from turning her back on the place in whose support her late husband had lost his life, his widow, Dame Jane, fully backed this decision. Again Elizabeth was asked, alongside "mainland" trustees including Dame Jane herself and Geoffrey Howe, to bring her local knowledge and enthusiasm to bear. Thereafter, for the whole life of the Trust, Elizabeth spent a great amount of time and effort seeking out good causes meriting support, whether a promising musician unable to afford an expensive instrument or an integrated school struggling to establish a library.

Her third great cause has been the Salvation Army. Those who see the Army only or mainly as the singers of fervent hymns or performers in rousing bands are unaware that it is the largest non-state provider of social services. Invited by Lucy Faulkner (widow of Northern Ireland's last Prime Minister) to join the local Advisory Board, Elizabeth became chairman in 1997, brought together a new organisation of Friends of the Salvation Army

(now more than a hundred strong and including two Nobel prize-winners), and over the years has persuaded inspirational speakers and musicians to offer their services gratis at numerous fund-raising events at such venues as Hillsborough Castle or Belfast City Hall. In this way, very large sums have been raised to support the Army's social work, much of it aimed at the most needy and unfortunate of our fellow-citizens.

From all of her experience and my own I have drawn two firm conclusions. The first is that the multiple needs of individuals can never be met, will never be met, by public sector action alone, and that the cumulative contribution of the voluntary sector is invaluable. The second is a moral conclusion. We will never be a wholesome and truly concerned society if we look to government to meet all our diverse needs. The voluntary commitment of individual people to wider communal ends ought to be a touchstone of our values. Margaret Thatcher, love her or hate her, was a remarkable person and leader in a great many ways. But no, Margaret, there is such a thing as society, and it ought to be a privilege to serve it.

We will
Remember
them

Report of the Northern Ireland Victims Commissioner,
Sir Kenneth Bloomfield KCB

April 1998

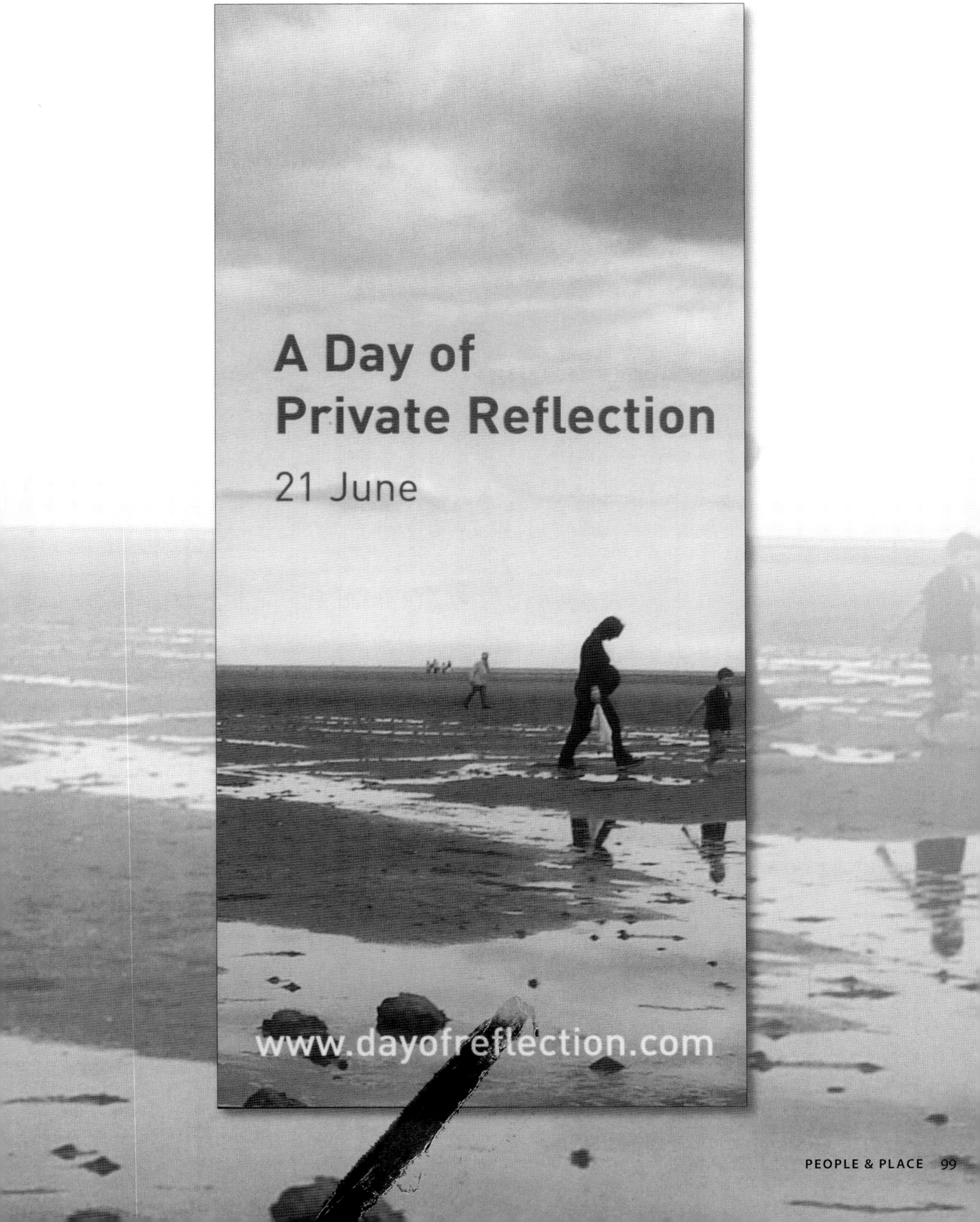

**A Day of
Private Reflection**

21 June

www.dayofreflection.com

FELICITY McCARTNEY *Community Activist*

'IN 1969 I RETURNED from two years overseas service in Ghana. I thought of going into VSB to see if I could volunteer for something locally. Niall Fitzduff had just started as the development officer. Mrs Peskett was in charge of VSB. They were keen to get the involvement of people who had done voluntary service overseas. There was a big meeting, and a lot of people were interested in volunteering locally.

The group – the 'return Volunteers Group' met throughout the winter of 1969 – 70, to discuss if volunteers were willing to do something, what they could do. The idea to have children's play schemes next summer came out of it – we didn't know how long the Troubles would be around for, but we'd a feeling they'd still be around. We had LTVs from various organisations such as the IVS and the Quakers work camps and the Corrymeela work camps and the Christian Movement for Peace. A number of organisations ... had work camps in NI – and we got them signed up for the children's play schemes around Belfast the next summer.

There was myself and David Bass and a few others who happened to be Quakers. We were allocated to Ballymurphy for the play schemes, and arranged to meet with Ballymurphy Tenants Association – a long standing group. It was a Belfast Corporation Estate – not as good as some of the other estates, there were rent strikes. It was very active with other tenants associations around Belfast – in some ways the first community network – the Belfast Amalgamated Corporation Tenants

> *I was brought up in Lurgan, not an upmarket place – very segregated. I didn't meet Catholics, who grew up in different areas.*

Association – it was keen to have a summer play scheme, keen to have something in the summer holidays. There were twenty volunteers – five locals – the rest from the Quaker work camp organisation in London, volunteers from Germany, Poland, and America.

We were allocated a couple of Americans – VSB acted as a 'clearing house' for volunteers from the Presbyterian Church in Seattle, and had a longstanding relationship with the Quakers. Helen Hunniman, who went on to Glebe House and the District Partnership in Down and Doug Baker worked up at Corrymeela, came through the work camps.

In Ballymurphy we were sleeping in the community centre on beds lent by the army. We'd get up in the morning to find lines of army with plastic shields – and stone throwing going on just outside the door. If there was rioting late at night, the next morning the children might not turn up until lunchtime.

The troubles were right there on the street – that was the summer of 1970. People were getting hostile to the army – it was hot and heavy in Ballymurphy. We would get the kids organised for bus trips – to beaches, to Castlewellan Park, Helen's Bay, Newcastle – we tried to go to places where there wasn't too much commercial amusement – instead we'd go for country walks and forest walks.

It was an open door – on the first day there were 300 kids – juniors, middles and seniors – kids hanging from the heights, we absorbed big numbers.

In these early days, looking back, we spent three weeks sleeping in the community centre, in two rooms – all the women in one room and all the men in the other – with a small kitchen. A volunteer was nominated as a cook – local people volunteered to come in and work in the kitchen. The Quaker camps would fundraise to get money to buy food.

I was brought up in Lurgan, not an upmarket place

Summer Playschemes 1970

VOLUNTARY SERVICE BUREAU
Bryson House Belfast

– very segregated. I didn't meet Catholics, who grew up in different areas. I was amazed at the cultural differences – say in funeral arrangements – how different it is in different parts of the country. I remember the first time I witnessed a funeral with an open casket was in Ballymurphy. I was used to the corpse in the bedroom and if you were close – like if it was a grandparent – you'd be taken to see them. In Ballymurphy, people grew up in smaller houses. They'd sit in a circle of chairs – have a cup of tea - with the coffin in the room.

The volunteers had a great time. They were right in the heart of west Belfast – I'm sure their parents were having fits. It was three weeks – in the era before mobile phones – and it was very much the beginning of the troubles. It's interesting – I'm still in touch with many of those volunteers to this day.

Summer outing 1970s. Photo: David Bass

MARIE ABBOTT *Summer Playschemes*

' I first came into contact with VSB in the summer of '73. I went to Bretton Hall college in Yorkshire in 1971. One of the men in the year above me – a drama student, was looking for people to come to Northern Ireland to do street theatre.

Doff Pollard had worked here and myself and another friend came to visit Jarvine Sillitoe, who was working in UHU, the travelling arts group. We hadn't come as volunteers, but she said they were short and needed help. We were sent to a play scheme in Turf Lodge.

There were about 200 kids every day – discos, trips away – helpers, local teenagers, teams of volunteers from elsewhere.

I stayed on for a year and got a full time job as a play leader for the Northern Ireland Adventure Playground Association. I stayed in touch with the people I met through my community work. Although I left in 1974, I came back in 1977. In the summer of '76 I met my future husband Paul in London – he was from Belfast.

Street Theatre 1973. Photo: Marie Abbot

I got a job in VSB at the end of that year as a part time training officer on the Lisburn Road. It involved training and arranging volunteer opportunities for placements, mainly for people at the start of their LTV year.

LTV's was a really interesting concept – the Long Term Volunteers were highly motivated young people thinking of careers in social work, youth work or teaching, It gave them a year's opportunity for experience. They were organised into area-based teams, with team leaders. These were Bill Osborne, Sheila-Jane Malley, now head of BBC Children in Need, Carole Graham, now with the Simon Community, and Brian Sheridan.

"They were team leaders – negotiating placements and I arranged the induction and general training for a range of volunteers,

I was at VSB about three years. It was a very dynamic, youthful organisation. Volunteers came from Northern Ireland, England, Scotland America – some are still working in Belfast – like Blanche Thompson, now Playworker in Belfast City Council.

There was a strong volunteer scene in the seventies. It was the impact of the troubles – people stayed very much in their own communities, and organised their own activities. I got a sense of how the troubles confined people to their own areas. I remember back in '73 looking for somewhere to live. People would say – 'don't go there, don't go here'- they had an acute sense of local geography and which areas were 'safe'.

During the Ulster Workers strike there were no buses. We had to get across town to work, and had to create a sense of normality to keep the playground facilities open – but it wasn't a normal time. '

KATE CAMPBELL *Summer Play Schemes*

' I worked in East Belfast – on the Woodstock Road – with other local volunteers. I had done a bit of youth work in Bangor when I was in my teens. I was arty too – studying at the art college, which was useful for summer schemes.

I left home at that time and never went back. We lived and stayed in the area, the group of us – and we would meet up with the other VSB volunteers every morning at Bryson House. It was very progressive – they would run morning yoga sessions for the volunteers. There was always something happening there – a real buzz, with volunteers from all over, from the United States, France – wherever! Most of us were away from home for the first time, so it felt quite exciting.

There were four of us in our group, all aged around twenty or twenty one, plus a teenage volunteer who was sixteen. We had an arts and crafts van, and travelled around Belfast in this van – full of art stuff, and learned what we were meant to be doing along the way! We had a rota for driving, and just got on with it – there was no such thing as health and safety back then. It would turn your hair grey now when I think about it.

We just went into what was a tough area on the Woodstock Road. We worked out of an old bonfire hut, getting fleas from the old furniture. I remember us comparing flea bites!

At that time the play scheme was based in a derelict house in Moore Street. The roof was leaking. The army had to put Perspex on the roof – which was fine as it let in some light.

Before the summer schemes got underway, we would travel around Belfast in our van, going to

Playscheme art 1970s style.

> *The voluntary commitment of individual people to wider communal ends ought to be a touchstone of our values.*

the schools and asking them for any art equipment that was left over at the end of the school year. We would end up with reams of paper. We took everything we could get from the art college at the end of the year too. We were the travelling artists – the kids thought we were art experts. Some of the group did go on to become acclaimed artists.

There was John Kindness – he's the artist who did the Big Fish on Belfast's Laganside. It's become something of an iconic landmark for Belfast. He started out as a VSB volunteer on the summer play schemes.

VOLUNTARY SERVICE BELFAST *Reports 1976-1977*

A guitar player on the doorstep of a derelict ... but ... two helpers ... the natural curiosity of children ... the ingredients of yet another holiday community play scheme for children in one of the many socially deprived areas of Belfast. The young volunteers of VSB are once more meeting a challenging need. This report is based on their reactions, their experiences.

In those days we would have got searched a lot. The soldiers at the check points would say 'We're watching you; we know you go across different areas'. They must have thought we were a bit suspicious because there weren't too many vans going across the whole city in those days.

With each summer scheme group we would build up to a grand finale at the end of the eight weeks. Poverty was a big issue for children in these areas. Most of houses didn't have their own bathroom; there were a lot of social problems. Yet these people welcomed us into their areas, they made us cups of tea, they took us into their own houses, they shared what they had with us and they made the effort to get to know us. There was myself, John Kindness, Philippa Brown, Danae Campbell and an English woman – Jarvine Sillitoe. I think they genuinely appreciated what we were doing, and they knew we were just a group of volunteers – although we did get £8 a week for what was called volunteer expenses. My rent was £1 a week back then! I'd spent my summer the year before working in a canning factory in England, and although I was making good money, it was no fun.

I can honestly say that working as a summer scheme volunteer back then was to shape me for the rest of my life – absolutely! Although I was at Art College, I'd trained as a youth worker in Bangor. The summer scheme shaped my future and my future career choices. I developed political awareness – not so much about the conflict, more of a social awareness – especially an awareness of poverty. It was the late sixties and early seventies and many, many people in Belfast were really poor.

But they were different times back then. I remember one local woman who got involved in the summer schemes – she was called Muriel. She would have to rush home in the early evening to light the fire and get her husband's tea ready – because he would complain if she hadn't it all done when he got home. He didn't approve of her helping out at the summer schemes. That was the position women were in back then. Men stood around on street corners and women were in the home with the children and tending to the men.

For me, it was a baptism of fire the first year I worked as a volunteer on the summer schemes. Yet I always felt supported so it must have been a good ship. ,,

M O O R E S T R E E T P L A Y S C H E M E

Hi!

We are two volunteers who will be on the Moore Street playground for the summer holidays, to try and help get some activities going for the children. We have a small programme already worked out, and hope to add to it. Suggestions will be greatly appreciated!

FACILITY	DATE	CENTRE OR PICK UP PLACE
Film Show	Tue., 11th July	10.30-11.30a.m. Cost 2p at 'Mitchells'
Minibus trip	Tue., 11th July	15 children from 10a.m. to 5 p.m. to destination of their choice. Cost 10p
Minibus trip	Thu., 13th July	15 children from 10a.m. to 5 p.m. to destination of their choice. Cost 10p
Single/decker bus	Mon., 17th July	35 children from 10a.m. to 5 p.m. Cost 10p
Ormeau Baths	Wed., 19th July	Transport at 1.30p.m. for 30 children. Cost 3p.
Travelling Theatre (including games, dressing up and plays)	Sat., 22nd July	Moore Street playground at approx. 2.15p.m.
Film Show	Tue., 25th July	10.30-11.30a.m. Cost 2p. at 'Mitchells'
Ormeau Baths	Wed., 26th July	Transport at 1.30p.m. - 30 children
Travelling Theatre	Sat., 29th July	Moore St. at approx. 2.15

Mother's help on single decker bus trip on 17th July would be greatly appreciated, please. More information about August to follow – look for posters in local shops.

We have got permission to use 11 Hamilton Place as an indoor Moore Street play centre, and hope to do arts and crafts there. So please could you keep a big bag or box in a corner of the kitchen and save any of these things...?

silver foil-milk bottle tops
polythene
tins andYogurt or cream cartons
wire
foam rubber
cardboard boxes

newspapers
scraps of material
egg boxes
plastic bottles
old clothes for dressing up

P.S. These things can be collected, if you let us know.

See you around. Come over and chat!

Katy and Yvonne

DANAE KINDNESS *UHU*

'My volunteer experience was in 1973 when I worked as part of a travelling arts group. I was sixteen.

I remember having written to VSB for an opportunity to do voluntary work over the summer, but hadn't heard anything. So I decided to call into the office and met a woman called Mena, one of the volunteer organisers. She asked me what I was interested in; I said I was interested in art. She said she could think of a project I could join – a travelling arts group. I was the baby of the group. The rest were at Art College.

There was a van used for the project. I can't recall the sequence of events. It was a hired van that had been used by an abattoir and had to be cleaned out. The van stunk slightly – there were maggots and things in it.

We were kitted out in white painters' overalls. This differentiated us going into these areas – there was a safety issue, of course there were issues at that time of strangers going into certain areas, locals were concerned if anyone different came in.

We were the UHU group – the name was intentional – because it was the name of a glue – it was about bonding together. The group as a whole maintained contact – we became firm friends; I made a connection with the people who became my mentors. There were five of us in the group – myself, Kate Campbell, Phillippa Brown, John and Jarvine – who went back to England. It was a slightly hippy group, we very much went with the flow. I'd have said yes to anything going, I would have gone along. We did go up to a place in Coleraine – a park. There was an aerial

UHU group 1973. Photo: John Kindness

The van stunk slightly – there were maggots and things in it.

jump. We got stuck with kids on top of the ladder – they wouldn't jump off, they were too frightened. We had to take one girl down. At that point I'd no fear – I remember jumping off the aerial run – a new experience.

I'd my first experience of some food I'd never come across before. I was asked would I eat spaghetti. I said yes thinking it'd be like spaghetti hoops – I didn't recognise it. A lot of people were in from England working as volunteers. All of these experiences were rich. It was a fantastic experience – a brilliant experience for me, and had a knock on effect.

When I think back, what a unique experience! How else would you have that experience – of incredible access and experience – in some ways it was a privilege. I was too young to really understand how privileged I was. When I look back, it is something I am very proud of. It was a unique time, a special summer.'

MAGGIE ANDREWS *Community Activist*

1970's Bouncy Castle inflatable. Photo: Marie Abbot

'I first got involved as a volunteer with the PHAB club at Fleming Fulton and the Dee Street Gateway Club which was attached to the adult day centre. I also helped at the Stranmillis Holidays in the summer time – a respite care programme organized directly by VSB and providing much needed support for carers. That was in 1975 – it allowed us an escape from our neighbourhoods for several days. We stayed in the Stranmillis Halls of Residence and everyone got involved in inter-generational activities, it was a great way to use the facilities outside term time and always attracted plenty of willing volunteers.

One of the best examples of community involvement to this day for me was the summer scheme at Ashmount Estate off the Holywood Road. Ashmount was known as Tintown because the houses were post war pre-fabricated bungalows. Members of the Tenants' Association offered their houses for lunchtimes to allow the volunteers to escape from the children for a while. They would make us tea or coffee (it was mainly tea in those days so we only had to bring our sandwiches). The young people would sit outside and wait for us to come out, we were like the Pied Piper!

Everyone in the neighbourhood made a commitment to and enjoyed the summer scheme. It was a small estate and there was a bus run to Portrush every year that almost everyone on the estate went to.

Inflatables were the new thing for summer schemes in those days and we had to go to Queen's University Students Union to make these 'bouncy castles'. A volunteer from Liverpool, Mike Jubb,

> *Being a volunteer isn't all about smiles. For this project I not only learnt how to 'deep clean' but acquired painting and decorating skills as well. All this at the age of 18 and still at school!*

brought the idea to Belfast. Mike and another volunteer called Trish Calvert were the brains behind these rubber creations, providing the patterns and the instructions. Part of the fun was that we had to get inside and we would emerge swooning from the smell of the glue. Needless to say there were plenty of breaks!

There was great entertainment and camaraderie in making these inflatables. All the volunteers were about the same age so we were able to make some lasting freiendships.

There was a derelict house in the middle of a terraced street off the Beersbridge Road which VSB decided to clean up and use as an after schools project and toy library. My recollection is that a person was violently killed in that house – a postman. Local people were very disturbed about what had happened and the house was a constant reminder.

What VSB did then was a bit like what is now

known as 're-imaging' – taking down unpleasant murals and replacing them with something positive. The period the house was used by local children allowed it to be seen differently before eventually it was lived in again.

I vividly remember how grim it was to clean the place out as the house was invested with cockroaches. Pest control was summoned and they just dusted around the skirting boards and we came the next day and literally shovelled dead cockroaches into bin bags. Being a volunteer isn't all about smiles. For this project I not only learnt how to 'deep clean' but acquired painting and decorating skills as well. All this at the age of 18 and still at school!

Colin Bowers and Pat Ryan were volunteers who also discovered hidden talents while they were volunteering. Pat came all the way from Minnesota to find out he really wanted to be a clown. Colin and Pat toured playgroups and children's projects in East Belfast as clowns – even appearing in the Daily Mail!

Streets where children play ..at their peril

BY ANNE FRY

"The children round here just don't have a chance," one mother told me. "They can't be kept in all the time and there's nowhere safe they can play." If they are playing outside, the mothers are constantly peering out of the windows, shouting and running to the front door to see the children are safe.

"My nerves are shattered," one woman said, "and if ever I hear the squeal of brakes, I'm terrified to run to the door in case its my child."

Two doors away from Stephen lives six year old Brian. One month after Stephen was injured, his cousin was crossing the road near her home. A taxi was speeding down the road and couldn't brake in time to avoid her. She landed on the roof and was hurled into the air.

"I heard the brakes screech," her mother told me. "then a neighbour rushed in to tell me there'd been another accident. I ran out and saw my little girl lying there unconscious. Her head was badly bruised, all her front teeth had been knocked out and there was a gaping hole in her leg."

That was six months ago. Jacqueline is better now, though she is still too nervous of traffic to cross the road by herself. "She was nearly killed and it almost killed me." said her mother.

Solutions

Various solutions to the road accident problem have been proposed, and a police spokesman suggested an inexpensive and effective remedy — the provision of a lay-by in every street.

Mrs. Joan Houston, superintendent of Shaftesbury Nursery School, stressed the urgent need for more nursery schools in the area. Her own school has a capacity for 75 and a waiting list of 150.

Parents collecting their children from the school told me of their relief at knowing their children are safe from traffic. Before the school opened they played a few feet away from heavy traffic on the dirty footpaths where many children are playing now.

Adventure playgrounds are another way of lowering the accident rate and the incidence of damage, accidental or otherwise. There, children can enjoy themselves without annoying old people causing damage to property.

The leader of Dee St. adventure playground said: "The children can use their own ideas and it doesn't matter if they break a window. They can really let off steam here."

Why can't more adventure playgrounds be built in Belfast? Well, cost is one factor, for the Adventure Playground Association is largely dependent on voluntary contributions. Another relevant factor is the availability of suitable sites.

Many children are now playing on pieces of waste land which serve a dual purpose; as playgrounds and rubbish dumps. One such site is in Tyne St. and the mother of a four-year-old girl who lives near it tells me, "people dump their rusty bikes and broken bottles there, and the site, a former housing site, has been in that condition since the last war."

Why can't places like this be cleaned up, fenced off and made into children's playgrounds?

The Corporation say that they make every effort to clean up such sites, dumping on waste land is a real problem. Offenders are prosecuted and new — tougher — legislation is now being considered by Parliament.

Sites can be made into playgrounds, subject to approval from the Education Committee.

Teachers and parents proposed another solution to the road safety problem: the provision of play streets in certain areas.

The executive officer of the Police Committee, Mr. Gordon Hayes, told me that a play street scheme was operated in Dee St. for a time, until residents there complained about the increased amount of noise.

Attitude

Play streets attracted children from surrounding areas and in all probability they would have to cross busy roads, to get there.

Mr. Hayes added that in certain Belfast streets, including Springview and Lancaster traffic had been restricted. They were, he said, aware of the particular problems facing Conway Street. The transportation study being carried out by the city's master planners was expected in May when decisions affecting the road system will then be made.

The solution to the road accident problem lies in the urgent provision of better playing facilities by the Corporation. Parents, too, must play their part by ensuring that their children know about road safety.

"You don't think an accident can happen on your doorstep. But it can happen — you can be involved."

The hub of volunteer activity in East Belfast was at a small house off the Woodstock Road – 3 Radnor Street. The house provided temporary accommodation for some of the many volunteers from across Europe and America that descended on Belfast at the time. It was where we all hung out and made plans – a brilliant outlet and opportunity for young volunteers in Belfast at a time when there were very few safe places to be. '

PAT RYAN *Summer Playschemes*

"How much?" I couldn't believe that a house I rented for £4 a month was now selling for £150,000. Bill and Wendy Osborne, my co workers from 30 years ago were showing my wife and me my old neighborhood in East Belfast. Yes, that's right, the terrace house I lived in 30 years ago had just sold for $300,000. Prosperity cannot always be judged in pounds or dollars but the value of property was just one of the shocks I was in for on my recent trip back to Belfast.

It was difficult for my wife to understand the world we worked in years ago. I was a long term volunteer with VSB in 1974. My area supervisor and my housemate was a gentleman named Stan Reid. Stan died in an accident in Scotland a few years after we worked together. Stan and a number of others were a great influence on me. The Belfast I came to love is better than ever with a lot fewer 'distractions'. It took me a while to get my bearings but soon I was back on the Woodstock Road and remembering my work with the playschemes, the deaf and my weekly calls on old age pensioners. Through all of it I remember most the people I worked with who day in and day out

Pat Ryan, Radnor Street, 1974

> *Belfast changed my life. I never looked on any situation the same after my year there.*

left the politics out of community work.

The unstated philosophy then and it seems to be the same today was "one small act at a time makes the difference". How we treated one another was as important as how we went about our work in the communities. We worked hard, we were conscientious and most of all we didn't take ourselves too seriously. It was the lowest paying job I ever loved. What we didn't get in our pay packets we got in laughs. Like the night I took a group of deaf kids to the Bay City Rollers concert. The kids loved the energy of the concerts and they could actually 'feel' the sound waves. There were a few scary times when the fans thought our mini bus with the Deaf Society logo on the side was a perfect cover for the band. They crowded around our van looking for the lads from Scotland. There was also the day my clown partner Colin and I were in our costumes and we arrived at a playbus only to be sent away because the kids were afraid of us. A passing military patrol posed no threat to them but a couple of clowns were terrifying.

Belfast changed my life. I never looked on any situation the same

Pat Ryan with Sandy Row coal merchants

after my year there. It taught me that there is always another story behind the story. The everyday efforts of good will do make a difference. Whether it's in South Africa, Bosnia or Palestine there are people who are there taking care of the business of caring for people.

I asked Maggie Andrews, a former VSB volunteer, how things were going and she said, "We don't worry about tomorrow we just take what we have today and today it's good. "

Colin, Stuart and Stan, Radnor Street.

MARY SPENCE *Summer Playschemes*

" In the summer of 1975, I was an 18 year old girl with great passion for theatre and had the opportunity to work as part of the Bing Bop Street Theatre. Having a strong connection to my Irish inheritance, I told my worried parents that I was going to Belfast for the summer to do street theatre at a time when the 'Troubles' were very apparent in the City Centre and many of the areas we performed, including Divis Flats. My experience there was undoubtedly one of the most formative of my young adult years and I have since gone on to become a

school psychologist, who continues to be involved with efforts to use theatre to help young people with autism improve their social-emotional skills. I credit Dr Ron Olauson of Mankato State University and Pat Ryan for my wonderful time in Belfast along with Aileen Herman, Stan Reid and my fellow Bing Bop players for an unforgettable experience.

I learned some great wisdom through those times and I try to apply it regularly in the work I do now in helping others, including how to deal with violence, difficult emotions and reconciliation. "

Photos: Marie Abbott

WENDY OSBORNE *Summer Playschemes*

'In 1974 I was 20. VSB was holding summer schemes across the city and was looking for volunteers for the summer months. I applied.

There were a lot of Americans and English – mainly young people aged around 19 and 20, who were interested in coming to Belfast for the summer.

I was placed in the Ormeau Road with Stuart from Basingstoke. He had 'John Lennon' glasses. He was living with some of the other volunteers in Brian Green's house. He went to live in a commune in Yorkshire afterwards.

There was also a volunteer who was the son of the Count and Countess of Alloa. I can remember him showing us his Coat of Arms. His family sent out a search party for him. He came back here year after year. Many volunteers who came here for a summer ended up staying.

Sadly Brian Green is dead now. He was a community activist in the Lower Ormeau Community Association – it was not called that then – with people like Joyce McCartan, who was later personally known to Hillary Clinton, and Dolores Rea.

At that time the place was full of bricked up houses – two up, two down. There was were community tensions, it was the height of the troubles.

There was tension between the Provos and Officials – inner tension and outer tension. It put pressure on the community - there was nothing for anyone to do – not even a playground.

There was no such thing as health and safety; I remember us kicking open a bricked up house. We wanted a community house so we could run a

> *I remember us kicking open a bricked up house. We wanted a community house so we could run a summer scheme.*

summer scheme. We didn't have any money but we had to find space. I knew nothing about Belfast at that time, it was a defining experience. Yet because it was a fresh experience, that led to it being a success.

That summer, in my mind, every day was sunny. We had no money so we had to use our imagination; we went to shops and asked for things, we went round and asked for ten tins of beans to take the kids camping. People got involved, even the shop keepers.

For the young children it was a great adventure to go out to Crawfordsburn Park – a lot of children never got out of their own area, but the parents knew nothing would happen to their kids.

We just used a piece of ground and a bricked up house. The children came from a small community that was made up of just a few streets in what is known as Lower Ormeau: McClure Street, Lavinia Street, Cook Street, Shaftesbury Avenue, Balfour Avenue.

I've never forgotten it, it was a volunteer experience that can change your life – because it was

Army patrol, Lower Ormeau Road. Photo: Brian Greene

Burning bus – Lower Ormeau. Photo: Brian Greene

outside your own personal experience, you begin to understand what a community can feel like under pressure. My experience in the Lower Ormeau road has stayed with me all my life.

There was a vibrancy around those volunteer schemes, but they were of their time.

There was tremendous inventiveness, energy – but things move on. Yet it really worked at the time, it worked for the volunteers and the communities.

There was a sense of camaraderie during the summer schemes, and there was a sense of loss when it finished. It was such a strong experience, it stays with you.

Stuart was a veteran community activist – he loved the way you could see the hills round Belfast. He would say 'how can there be any trouble when you can see the hills?'

Things move on. It's much more sophisticated now, but the play schemes provided something when there was nothing; and the communities welcomed them.

There was always a watchful eye and strong support from the community - even in that bricked up house – you felt supported by the community.

That whole experience gave me confidence. After that summer I went into the Ulster Museum and asked to volunteer; that was something I'd always wanted to do. I thought if I can do that in the Lower Ormeau, then I can do that in the Ulster Museum.

I've volunteered with the Church and youth clubs since 15, then at university with the community action group. After 1974 I remained a serial volunteer interested in causes and communities. I like to get involved.

You meet so many people through volunteering that you wouldn't meet if you didn't get involved.'

Lower Ormeau Summer Playscheme 1974 – visit of street theatre. Wendy Osborne and Margaret Clinton in the background (right)

MARGARET CLINTON *Summer Playschemes and Playbus*

'I was 15 in 1974 when I volunteered for the summer scheme on the Lower Ormeau.

My mother was asked to do something with the younger teenagers to help stop the rioting. It was a bit like early peer mentoring with young people from the area. Some of these people would still be involved in youth work. Sometimes whole families would be involved. Volunteers are bred – my mum was involved in the local community. If your mum did it, the kids did too; you learned to give back to your community. I was involved in the toy library for the next 25 years.

It just goes down generation to generation – especially if you live in a close area, volunteering is the heartbeat of those areas. Back then, people wanted to help themselves; they said 'we need to make this better'.

At that time, on the summer schemes, there would have been a lot of English people working as volunteers – and obviously, speaking with English accents. It let the people in the area see that not all English people wore a uniform; that they are not just there to go into your house in the middle of the night...

I work for Sure Start now – it's about empowering women. In the seventies there were a lot of strong women in these communities; then that filters down through other generations. It was a matriarchal society; the women were the heartbeat of the communities; the real activists.

They were strong and scary women. If there was any trouble there were four mummies coming up the street with their arms folded, and any bother stopped straightaway. They were very strong, and they knew what they wanted for their children.

Orange Parade, Lower Ormeau Road. Photo: Brian Greene

Donkey and cart with kids and the VSB Playbus. Photo: Brian Greene

I remember my mummy going up to Stormont on a protest with a cow! My mum and Joyce McCartan and Brian Green's wife took a cow up to Stormont to protest at the milk being taken away from the schools.

They were good times – people opened their doors. If someone had to find a bed, the community found them a bed. Now it's all geared at money; I think we were more resourceful – we would take the breeze blocks out of bricked up houses.

On the Ormeau Bridge it was open warfare until the summer schemes came. They were nicknamed 'the community relations police'. When the parades were going down the Lower Ormeau, everyone who lived there paraded off to Newcastle for the day, to make it clear for the parades.

There were buses and buses went off to Newcastle on 12th July. No one came home dry; everyone went – all the mummies, daddies, teenagers and kids, and everyone would come home soaked. Piles and piles of sandwiches were made, juice bottles filled – and we went off on the buses, then you ended up coming home on a different one. You would get on one of the buses and shout 'do you recognise everyone?'

When you'd arrive back home, the bands were away; and so were the tensions. It was of its time – you probably couldn't do that now. That time has passed, but it was all part of the experience of volunteering.

I lived in McClure Street until I was 17. During the day, everyone's door was open; it was a sign of the times. Stuart was from a small mining village in England – he'd say the people there were just the same. Even though Belfast is a city, it's like a village – everyone relates to everyone.

In all the years I did the summer schemes, I never had to complain to anyone's mummy. We took children to North Wales, Glencree, Newcastle, Corrymeela. If there was any bother I just said 'I'm telling your mum' and that was the end of it.

After the summer schemes and Playbus I got involved with the Toy Library. I did that in October 1978 along with the play buses. We brought educational toys and books to children in their communities. We converted an old bus. It's now in the Ulster Transport Museum.

As a long term volunteer I got £16.20 a week – £1 more than you got on the brew.

At one stage I had lumps all over my body; it turned out they were bug bites. Mum threw a plastic bag at me and said 'stand out there and scrub yerself...'

It's 35 years ago since that first summer I volunteered. It gave me confidence to speak out. It gave me a different perspective – to see loads of different lifestyles. Everyone had their own problems – you mightn't have the same outlook, but no one came with that.

Lower Ormeau Playscheme – day trip to Newcastle. Photo: Brian Greene

Lower Ormeau Playspace Rally. Photo: Brian Greene

DONAL McKEOWN *Auxiliary Bishop, Down and Connor*

'My background in volunteering starts in Randalstown where I grew up in the 50s and 60s. There was a strong sense of community identity – with evening classes, hurling, Gaelic, dancing. It was that type of environment. I had a substantial family circle – if you spit on one we all sizzle.

I went to Queen's University in 1968 and got involved in community things – and VSB was the largest of those things. I stayed in Belfast at the weekends and some of us thought 'what can we do?' We were sent out to do work for people in their houses.

I recall on one occasion being in the Oldpark Road area, decorating a house for an old couple. They were nice people. In the room there was all these loyalist and unionist flags. We went up there to work one day and the next day heard that a body had been dumped in the street. We were around eighteen to twenty then – and were foolhardy, but thought that this might not be the best place for names like Donal and Vincent to be at that time...

> ### I had a substantial family circle – if you spit on one we all sizzle.

Around Carlisle Circus, we were decorating a house for an old lady. There was a big hole in the living room floor. The floor was put in and we were decorating the house and dumped a lot of old rubbish. She was on to VSB complaining that someone had stolen 'all her good clothes'. They had been dumped in Newtownabbey. We had to go up there and haul out the rubbish that had been dumped the previous evening. We told her it had been brought to St Vincent de Paul but we got it back before it was snapped up quickly!

Girl at Farringdon Gardens. Photo: Stanley Matchett

My days with VSB are full of memories. I did other things as a student – as a volunteer with St Vincent de Paul. There was Knockinelder at Portaferry – a St Vincent de Paul house. Kids from Belfast would go there for holidays. They were innocent days – my mother would come and cook – we were well watered and fed. They would play football, or would be sent

> ### Volunteering was an outlet for that energy and idealism. For university students, it was part of the educational experience.

down to the big beach – you wouldn't think of it now.

The culture of volunteering was part of life's experience. There were riots in Ardoyne. Farringdon Gardens was burnt down. Sean Cooney – he died recently – we were asked to help to clear out the burnt houses.

There was the curfew in the Lower Falls in the early seventies. A group of us volunteered to go round and take statements. Our Central Citizens' Defence Committee passes meant we were not regarded as agents of the state. We had no money to entertain ourselves then – you had to entertain yourself, and volunteering was an outlet for that energy and idealism. For university students, it was part of the educational experience.

I was very thankful for the opportunities I got from VSB – we were a few country boys up in the big city. Voluntary work was not a burden, it was good fun. Time flew by. It was part of growing up and part of our education. It's healthy – it nourishes the human spirit. Anyone can make a contribution – from cleaning floors, doing odd jobs, or just spending time with people. There is a lot of loneliness out there, a lot of suicide. Through volunteering you can be supportive, but not intrusive.

You can't have a healthy community with a spirit of responsibility for one another without volunteering. There wouldn't be youth clubs, or

> *You can't have a healthy community with a spirit of responsibility for one another without volunteering.*

sports clubs, if it wasn't for volunteers. Too many expect others to do it. We wouldn't have an amateur sports world – so many sports just would not happen – without volunteers. The GAA, soccer clubs, rugby clubs, boxing clubs – all run by people prepared to put something into society.

Volunteering is not just a 'nice' thing. It builds social cohesion, anyone can contribute to social capital – to have pride, cohesion, to hold the community together.

Guest speakers at the official opening of Rosemount House, an alcoholism treatment centre on the Antrim Road in North Belfast, are centre Vice-Chariman Charlie McGarry, Mgr Joseph Chambers, centre Chairman Malachy Turley and Bishop Donal McKeown, Auxiliary Bishop of Down and Connor. Irish News, 24 May 2007.

ANIA KOSTYSZYM *European Volunteer Service*

'I have been in Belfast for nearly two years now. I came as an European Volunteer Service (EVS) volunteer in July 2006 and finished in April 2007, then I went back home to Poland for a holiday.

I came to Belfast when I finished my study in Management and Marketing at the Maritime University in Gdynia, on the north coast of Poland.

I started to travel a bit and I really like to visit as many places as I can – but most of my travelling until then had been with my parents and a tour guide, not on my own.

During my studies I was a part of the European Union Science Circle, where we would talk about the EU and the projects that enabled us to be a part of the European Union and to do a lot of travelling, and from this I got to know about the EVS programme. I decided to finish my study and think about doing this project.

I looked the programme up on the internet and found this project and so I started to research everything. That took a few months and involved lots of applications and sending CVs. Unfortunately most projects were already full, so I had to wait my time.

What attracted me to Belfast? I hadn't been here before and I wanted to improve my English. I just thought it was a good idea to come here. In my memories, people have the impression that it's still not attractive or safe, but it is a good place to live and the people are very kind. If I have any problems they help me.

I was curious a bit, and my parents were a little anxious, but they knew if I had an EU project place it would not be too dangerous. So I arrived in July 2006 with the EVS scheme.

It had two houses of EVS people – a lot of mixed nationality - close to the Ormeau Road. In my first house I shared with four different people and I was made very welcome and soon felt part of it.

At the beginning, when I arrived, I had a few days introduction. Mary Hegarty took me around Belfast in her car. It was my first time in Belfast so there were so many things to take in – the culture, the language, the history – things like that.

I remember a few days of introduction then I was straight in here – to Shopmobility. At the beginning I found the accent completely different form the English I had leant, but I began to discover it.

After a month I got to know my job and my tasks, and step by step I became more involved. I got to know more people, and became a part of the organisation that is Shopmobility.

What sort of tasks was I doing? Writing press releases, organising events, organising the volunteer forums. I also update the website and create the leaflets and posters. I participated in rambles which gave me a chance to visit many beautiful venues of Northern Ireland.

EVS is a nine month programme, but after my time Ann Collins offered me a job so I could stay here. I went to Poland for a holiday and came back to Belfast – it just happened like that.

The other EVS volunteers – I know that some stayed in Belfast and got a job and are, so far, enjoying their time here, some went back to their home countries. My EVS year really gave me more knowledge of different people, a different culture so that I became a more tolerant person.

What I like about Belfast is that there are so

> *What I like about Belfast is that are so many different people from so many different traditions, religions, and countries.*

many different people from so many different traditions, religions, and countries. We don't have that in Poland. There is more variety here and so much to experience.

The future? I haven't made up my mind yet. Back in Poland, it is a different country, for now I am happy here. I am quite an adventurous person and so I like travelling and staying in different countries. Where I am my new friends become my friends and my family. The other EVS volunteers, my colleagues from Shopmoblity – and people like Mary Hegarty, became my family here.

GERALDINE REID

I was seventeen and I wasn't working, I was a bit down and my doctor referred me ... or rather suggested ... that I go to VSB. I worked as a volunteer from 1978–79 in North Belfast – I remember running around the office signing "Busy doing nothing, busy the whole day through..."

I was from Ligoniel. Back then people stayed in their own areas – it was like a collection of ghettos. But the VSB volunteers came from all over the place and went anywhere. On a Friday afternoon we'd go to the Club Bar – it's now called The Globe. It was popular with bikers. I met loads of really interesting people – people from different countries.

It was a social outlet for people from different backgrounds – with atheistic views, or a strict Catholic background, or Protestant backgrounds. We were an eclectic bunch of young people thrown together.

I volunteered on the Play Schemes at Ballynafeigh and for old people when they did the holidays at Queens Elm's and in Bangor. I was also a volunteer on the residential Children's Holiday Schemes.

The positive side of volunteering is that I went into a lot of areas, worked with a lot of people and a lot of different groups.

MARY FRANCES BLANEY

In June 1985 I'd just finished school and wanted to do some voluntary work over the summer.

I was from South Belfast and ended up in parts of Belfast that I never even knew existed. It was 1985, the Troubles were still going on, and I saw things I'd never have seen unless I was in those areas.

I learned a lot about myself and my city and who I was. I hadn't realised there was no much poverty in Belfast – it opened my eyes. That summer helped me form in my mind what I wanted to do with my life. I was only seventeen. I look back on that summer with great fondness.

I did social work at college and in my final year I decided to work on the summer schemes.

Leaving York Road train station for Whitehead.

The summer schemes of 1987 involved groups of children aged from seven to thirteen or fourteen from both sides of the community – twenty Catholic and twenty Protestant children.

We would meet up at Yorkgate train station and take the train to Whitehead where there were lots of activities laid on. I'd done my life saving certificate while I was at College and there was an outside pool there. I really enjoyed that summer – with kids who had literally never met someone from the other side before. It was amazing to watch them begin to realise that they didn't have forked tongues and tails. They began a common realisation – 'Hey, he's just like me!' They began to realise there's more to life than sectarianism. That was important groundwork back then.

After that summer I got a full time job and my voluntary work sort of drifted away. I wasn't doing as much as I'd like. I was working with the older people's residential unit at Breda Park off the Saintfield Road.

I now work with people with learning difficulties at St John of God in Dublin – adults with learning disabilities and challenging behaviour.

My voluntary work was the stepping stone, the building block for the rest of my life. At the time I was just having fun – I didn't know how much it had impacted on me.

> *My voluntary work was the stepping stone, the building block for the rest of my life. At the time I was just having fun – I didn't know how much it had impacted on me.*

FIGHTING FOR THE COMMON GOOD

AND THAT HAS MADE ALL THE DIFFERENCE…

A personal reflection by Duncan Morrow

The beautiful thing about doing something because you choose to, is that there is nobody left to blame. Sure, there is probably someone or 'someones' who led you to the edge of choice, but the great thing about choice is that the last step, or is it the first step, is always yours. There is probably no greater freedom, than to know that the choices made were free and not forced.

I first realised this when I went as a volunteer to Austria on a Quaker project where we were to work with people with learning disabilities. I had chosen to go after University, because it seemed more exciting than any of the careers that were beckoning. But it was only after I left, that I saw that the whole experience had only been possible because I knew and accepted that I had chosen to go. Because of that, I did not mind doing long hours, or getting to know the people as friends and not clients. Because nobody had forced me, I never felt sorry for myself nor wasted time trying to climb the career ladder. I was just 'there', and could give as much or as little as I wanted. And because the people I was with set no limits, it was usually better to give more, because that was how you got the most back. By the end of it, a project in which

I had set out to 'help' the poor and needy of the world, had turned into one of the most totally accepting and moving experiences of my life.

These days, I get paid to work and talk and think about ways to make genuinely human relationships possible in the midst of the anger, resentment and fear that still drives division in Northern Ireland. But I still feel as if I am a volunteer who happens to be paid enough to feed his family. My first steps in what now goes by the name of community relations work, were to live in community with others in Corrymeela looking after groups of school kids, old people, families with all sorts of difficulties or just students. Differences of one sort were set aside, so that the deeper differences, the differences which meant that one person was sporty while another was good at sitting talking to people, could surface. Sure, the one was Catholic, the other Protestant or even German or American, but the work and the ethos gave us the space to suspend judgement until we met each other while looking after each other and stepping up to the responsibilities required to keep things going. They gave, I gave – we got. The rhythm of giving and receiving, which is the hidden secret of volunteering struck deep roots.

It left me with the deep imprint that the rules of culture could not be allowed to come between me and the human beings around me. So I set about volunteering to do something about it. Politically, things were always difficult. But change does not require the permission of a political leadership before you can take steps. The beauty of volunteering is that because you don't have to change everything, you can make a contribution even if success might seem limited, because it is freely done, not a chore. And if it looks like hard work, the real secret is, that I could not have it any other way. The visible giving has been more than matched by the ridiculous amount I have got back in friends, experiences and learning.

Change in Northern Ireland will not come because people are forced to love each other. It will happen because we recognise each other as people who need to be honoured, not because we have to but because it makes us more human. That can only happen if people take real steps. Somebody has to show the change not just talk about it. Doing will always be more real than talking, and offering to do things together will be even better.

After that kind of experience, nobody will ever go back to the simple slogans of 'them and us'.

There is a lot of talk in community relations work of 'dialogue'. Meeting to talk is important. But meeting to do together and be together is much more convincing, because the doing brings us into new situations with one another, where we see and hear differently. If we are to have a shared future, we will need much more places to be together, so that in the end we do it because it is what makes life worth living. Sometimes we may be paid for it, but it won't last unless it reflects that pattern of what we truly want. That's what will make the difference.

Photos: Corrymeela Community

Freemans is sponsoring 19-year-old David Thompson to work for 12 months in strife-weary Ulster. He is attached to Belfast's Voluntary Service Bureau, whose work includes distributing essentials in the city and surrounding districts. Assistant editor Mary McDowell visited Belfast to talk to David about his work.

The quieter struggle in battle-torn Ulster

'TRYING to help those least able to help themselves' — David communicating with a group of deaf people.

A BRIEFING with the director.

IN TROUBLED, battle-scarred Belfast, a pensioner waged a battle of his own. It involved his house — home to him for years — which, like many of its vacant neighbours, was becoming derelict. Damp patches covered the walls, the wallpaper was peeling, and he couldn't afford to make the necessary repairs.

He decided not to pay any more rent until the landlord carried out repairs. The landlord, however, threatened legal action and eviction for his troublesome tenant.

Unsure of his rights, afraid of what the landlord might do, he was on the point of giving up. Then a stranger stepped into the picture.

David Thompson is 19 and works for Belfast's Voluntary Service Bureau. He pointed out to the landlord that the pensioner was legally justified in withholding his rent and could use the arrears to pay for repairs. David then set the wheels in motion for the work to be done.

That pensioner is a lot happier now and he, like many others, has discovered someone to whom he can turn for advice, help or just company.

That's basically what VSB is all about. "We try to help those who are least able to help themselves — the old, sick, handicapped," says director Sidney Stewart.

The Bureau was born seven years ago. It started as a clearing house for furniture — collecting from charitable people and delivering to those in need.

Holidays

As the troubles in Northern Ireland escalated so did the services offered by VSB. As well as the growing furniture service, it is now involved in arranging holidays for pensioners who can't afford, but need them, after years of community strife; operating play-schemes for children living in deprived areas; decorating homes of the elderly or needy; assisting in clubs and day centres for pensioners and the handicapped, and much more.

There are 20 long-term volunteers like David who work under three field officers. Volunteers are paid a subsistence allowance of £12.50 a week — 75 per cent comes from the Government and the rest from interested individuals and firms like Freemans.

Our volunteer, David, joined VSB to discover if he could cope with the pressures of social work. "I've always wanted to be a social worker and this year will help me decide."

He works in South-West Belfast which includes notorious areas such as the Falls Road, Andersonstown and Ballymurphy. Yet he has never run across any trouble. "The possibility is always there, of course, but I don't let it worry me."

Since joining, David has dealt with about 200 cases referred to VSB mainly from social workers or good neighbours.

"Many people are just unbearably lonely and need someone to visit them. Others need a grant for decorating, and also a volunteer to do the job. Many people don't know who to contact if a pipe bursts. I've made doctor's appointments, taken housebound pensioners for a drive, and helped families to move house."

And all these VSB activities are linked by a thread which is rare in Belfast these days. Nobody is barred from help on grounds of religion or politics.

Thanks

David admits there are frustrations. "It's depressing much of the time, especially seeing the conditions many people are forced to live in. But there is a great feeling of satisfaction when you close a file on a case knowing you've done everything you can to help. And, occasionally, someone will ring to say thanks — that really makes my day.

"I suppose I am dedicated," he says. "But I don't want to bore people telling them about all the 'good' work I'm doing. It's my job. It has to be done and I might as well do it as anyone."

All this leaves David little time for his hobbies — canoeing, and singing in the Cathedral choir in his home town of Lisburn, just outside Belfast.

When his year is finished he hopes to become a trainee social worker. Meanwhile he carries on with work which won't solve Ulster's problems, but which means a great deal to many people.

As he points out: "We can't deal with the big, big problems. We leave those to experienced social workers. VSB tries to solve the little troubles to help make life a bit more bearable, a bit happier."

(David will be writing periodic reports on his work for Freemans News in future.)

PRACTICAL help too . . . David and another volunteer, Sharyn Preece, redecorating.

CHAOTIC DAY at Freemans Peterborough warehouse? . . . No, it's the Voluntary Service Bureau's furniture store in Belfast.

Article from the Freemans News, May 1975

ANON *(for Harry Trainor)*

'It was the early part of the troubles – around June – July of 1969 and I suppose I was excited stupidly in some way by what was happening in Andytown. There were refugees from the bottom end of the Falls due to arrive to set up makeshift homes in the gym of De La Salle school.

Harry Trainor – now deceased God rest him – was the prime mover in getting the school opened. He rounded up girls and boys aged around sixteen to seventeen to help.

Families were going into the school for refuge and each family needed to have an area of the gym designated to them. They got makeshift beds from the De La Salle brothers on the Glen Road.

Harry was a teacher at De La Salle and was well known in the area. He would try to push young people in the right direction – about morals, theology, going to Mass.

My memory of that summer was making babies' bottles in the school kitchens in the middle of the night. For several weeks, families and young children were living in the school gym. They had nowhere else to go. The prime mover in making that happen was Harry Trainor.

After three or four days it began to get media and press attention. Harry didn't take any of the limelight.

That summer the violence broke out and families were burnt out of their homes from the Falls, the Peace Line, Ardoyne.

Those families were housed in several schools – St Teresa's on the Whiterock Road for example. We

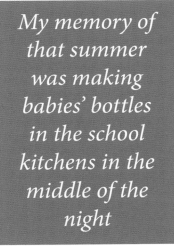

My memory of that summer was making babies' bottles in the school kitchens in the middle of the night

were aware as young people – metaphorically – of this explosion of events: the trouble, the brewing riots on the interfaces.

We knew these families were coming because they had nowhere else to go. Harry rounded us up to help unload their belongings and find them a living space in the gym and close to the school kitchen.

There were about twenty families, most with very young children and with babies.

As the summer wore on, the authorities managed to clear the school gym (it had to re-open as a school in September), mainly into vacant flats and houses in Lenadoon. They put up around ten or so temporary mobile homes in the playing area opposite. It later became known as Silver City – a huge army base.

The events of that summer – and the swift and selfless actions of Harry Trainor – were to have an impact without a doubt on me. I got a different perspective on the Troubles. Harry was very influential in a positive way.

He was a young teacher – only a few years older than us – but he'd stop and chat to you on the street corner. He would advise you – he was very Christian – but in a quiet way.

It was all very exciting for us but for the families that had been displaced it must have been very stressful.

There would have been around two dozen young people working with Harry as volunteers that summer. Harry organised a rota and we did shift work – making pots of tea, bottles, minding children, talking to people. It was real voluntary work – yet it was the most enjoyable summer – really helping people in need.

By September it had reverted to being a school. Harry was still to be found in and around the area, chatting to us, advising and guiding us.

I went on from there and got a degree and became a teacher too. But I learned so many things that

It was real voluntary work - yet it was the most enjoyable summer - really helping people in need

summer – I learned how to make a baby's bottle and how to use a sterilised needle to widen the teat.

He was only 22 when he did this most selfless thing, and showed so many young people why volunteering to help people in need was a good thing. It was a terrible injustice that he died from leukaemia, aged just 33.

Photo: Gerry Collins

BILL LOGAN *The Royal Black Institution*

' I have always been involved in the Loyal Orders and involved in the 'Black' since 1950.

The Royal Black Institution - being conservative with a small 'c' - didn't get involved in high profile things. We were not political – but in the late sixties there was trouble brewing around the 12th July 1969 – from the Carrick Hill and Peter's Hill area to the Shankill. This area is now generally known as Unity Flats. On 12th July the men were coming back to go up to the Shankill, stones were being thrown at them.

On the first Saturday of August 1969 the Junior Number One Orange District walked – children as young as seven or eight up to seventeen. The children would go on a day out with the band to Carrickfergus by train. They walked down over Peter's Hill past Unity Flats to York Street Rail Station, then proceeded to Carrick for the day.

I was an insurance agent at the time. I covered up the Shankill to Tennant Street. Every Saturday morning I walked from the Lower Shankill to Peter's Hill, Gardiner Street, Brown Street, Boyd Street – all adjacent to Unity Flats.

I went down that morning as usual to do my work and was told that there might be some problems. I spoke to some people and there was a bit of tension in the air. A neighbour of mine on the Ballygomartin Road, was a Sergeant in the RUC. He said there was a 'possibility of some difficulties here tonight, if you can do anything about it'. I telephoned a few responsible people from the Orange and the Black organisations and told them there could be some difficulties in the evening when the Junior Orange procession returned from Carrickfergus.

We got the children up along Royal Avenue. We walked on up North Street and there was a large crowd. We used our umbrellas to protect the

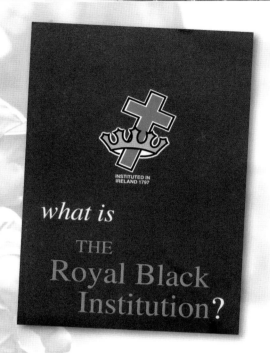

what is

THE
Royal Black
Institution?

INSTITUTED IN
IRELAND 1797

children from the stones. We got cleared from the area by 6.30 and returned home, but were horrified to learn that later that night there had been looting and rioting on the Shankill Road.

This appalled me. This was not the people of the Shankill Road that I knew, whose homes I went in and out of doing my business. It seemed that an unruly element had taken control.

On the Sunday night I couldn't sleep. I got up at 4am and prepared a statement. I felt it should be issued on behalf of the organisation. I got in touch with the Master of Nine District Orange, and said that things are bad, and that we as organisations had to do something. So we called a joint meeting of both the Black and the Orange Districts and agreed that this Trouble could not be allowed to continue, that we should try to bring a sense of stability. A further statement was issued, saying this was not the way the Shankill Road people should act. We sent copies of the statements to the Belfast Telegraph and the Newsletter which both gave extensive positive coverage of the peace keeping efforts being made.

A further meeting was held on the Tuesday night, when we asked our members to patrol the road and settle the people. There was a substantial turnout – 350 men came to the Orange Hall at 7.30 for the meeting and then went down the road in groups of three and four to talk to people in the side streets and help create a semblance of peace. It took the tension out of the air. Our purpose was to try to prevent people from going down to Unity Flats as the tension might escalate. The people of the Unity Flats were entitled to a peaceful existence. We were a group of people who were concerned about our own community. On that occasion good sense prevailed. But black or orange collarettes don't protect you from lead flying around on 13th and 14th August when the army came in and the Troubles began across Belfast.

There were hundreds of men, genuine decent men of the Shankill Road, members of the Orange and Black, who felt it was their responsibility. We had a high level of success, and earned a lot of respect for what we did in the area on the 5th and 6th August 1969.

A more detailed and perhaps more accurate description of the events of early August 1969 are detailed in my evidence to the 'Scarman Tribunal' on 3rd and 4th August 1970.

The contribution of the people of the Shankill Road continued for many years after that. There were difficulties and times of high tension, there was the trauma of bombs and bullets. In the early 1970s there were unnecessary murders. At particular times of possible tension our groups came together. We had a network of telephone numbers in the event

> *my wife Dorothy would say there are three of us in this marriage – you, me and the Black.*

of any local problems arising, we would come down and try to calm the situation.

One night, at Snugville Street Corner, there was a crowd gathered. Men pulled the timber fencing down and made a barricade further down at the corner of Moscow Street. The army – 'the paras' – were ready to move from the corner of Northumberland Street and Agnes Street up the Shankill. At 3am in the morning I got a call from Stormont, from Desmond Boal, MP, QC together – with others – we spent the night on the road and helped to cool the situation.

Late on Saturday afternoons on the Shankill Road, the Linfield supporters would be coming home from the match. A number of us would escort the supporters past the flashpoint area so that trouble would not erupt.

For several years a lot of people of the Shankill helped with that – I was not a prime organiser, but that was what people did to calm tensions and help to create a sense of stability for what was a proud people and a proud road.

What happened after August 1969, other elements took hold. Many people like myself were disregarded. My reason d'être for what I did was to keep my people from becoming involved in trouble.

Since then, I've moved on from my involvement in the Shankill District. I was Assistant Sovereign Grand Master for three years to Lord Molyneaux. In December 1998 I was elected by the membership to Sovereign Grand Master, and have held that position since.

The Royal Black Preceptory is a volunteer organisation – my wife Dorothy would say there are three of us in this marriage – you, me and the Black. ,

OWEN MAGUIRE *John Paul II Youth Club*

'VSB was involved in a way from the very beginning of this story – by running a summer scheme on the battle field of Ardoyne in 1971 and 1972. At that time young people weren't getting a chance to meet up. They were kept in the house. VSB organised a trip to Ballycastle and my late wife was involved in that. She went and had a great time.

The women formed a committee, and met in each others houses. There was lots of talk and the kids would be listening to what was going on.

There was a four storey house at the corner of Enfield and Herbert Street. It had been a shop way back but it was derelict. They took it over, under Sydney Stewart's direction, and with Fr Fernando from the church.

The boys from the local school did most of the bricklaying – the 16 year olds in their final year. They got stuck in. We got some money from Tom Fleming to buy cement. The idea was to fix it up, hold discos, put in a snooker table, that sort of thing.

At that time there was another youth club, a church youth club. When it closed we were inundated.

For the next five years I was a full time volunteer – from early to mid-seventies. I loved what I was doing, and applied to VSB for a full time position, and ended up taking it.

In 1977 to 1978 I went to Jordanstown and did a part time diploma in Youth and Community Work, and qualified in 1980.

Around 1978 we got a quarter of a million from Belfast Area Need and Lord Melchett for the new club, and we laid the foundations for the John Paul II Youth Club on Brookfield Place. We called it that because that was the year the Pope came to Ireland. It was to be a flagship for youth work, and our volunteering ethos was very strong. I retired

Lord Melchett speaking at a conference. Photo: Youth Action

two years ago and Jackie took over as manager. The managers have youth and community work degrees. I'm the chair – and still do a lot of voluntary work there. It always had that ethos of volunteering. Over the years a lot of things threatened its existence, and at times it was hard going, but we worked hard.

We lost a volunteer back in the Troubles. A young lad called Gerard Stitt. He was travelling down the Crumlin Road on a bus to give blood when he was shot in the head. Then there was another lad helped out, Paddy McKenna, he was shot at the top of the Crumlin Road.

In those days there was forever rioting on the Crumlin Road round the peaceline. On a Friday night we had our junior discos. I remember one night the paras banging down the door, and my wife stood across the door to protect the children.

We get great feedback all the time. The big thing that comes out is the people involved here. They say 'if it hadn't been for the club and the people in it, we'd be in jail right now.' We have heard that thousands and thousands of times since the beginning.

We were always available in the seventies and the eighties. We were open seven days a week, and we never got holidays. If we did get away, we usually had half a dozen young people away with us.'

LEEANNE DONAGHY *Charity Shop*

'I'm now 22 – I've been a volunteer with Save the Children for six years. I tidy up the shop. I'm in charge of the music department and keep everything in order. I check the dates are right, tidy up the clothes rack, empty the large bags, serve at the till, help customers with queries. Some will ask for different shoe sizes – 'have you got this in a six?' Some will ask us to measure up curtains or ask us to measure men's trousers!

It can be very entertaining. I deal with senior citizens, children – people from every walk of life. It's busy on a Saturday.

I have been in other Save the Children shops too – in Botanic Avenue in Belfast and the one in Cookstown. I have done hundreds of volunteer hours.

Customers ask silly questions. I help serve customers at the till – they ask for curtains, hats, silly things and I have to say no we don't have it. We get a lot of requests for men's braces – for fancy dress for parties – masks, dressing up clothes. We keep a box in the back with all that stuff in it.

Treat them well and with respect, they'll come back and say thank you.

I do the till, tidy up bric-a-brac and price it, tidy the rails, check it's all priced right. Sometimes customers take tags off you know, and when we put clothes out they pull the tags off. We don't tell the customers we know they've pulled it off. They are trying to get it cheaper. They pull the tags off bric-a-brac, shoes, clothes, books – books are a set price so we know.

Leeanne making a sale. Photo: Rory Moore

Here's a good one – customers do all sorts of things in charity shops. They would steal a shoe – then come back for the other one. Jane Shilton shoes are dear – you can buy them new in Menary's in Bangor, we take them in a lot. They know the makes – the customers.

Hopefully they come back – you have to build good will. Treat them well and with respect, they'll come back and say thank you. Keep the customers happy or they'll not come back.'

JIM McDONALD *Prince's Trust*

' My first volunteer experience was in the boy scouts – that was a very, very long time ago. When I got the chance I joined the Order of Malta as a volunteer first aider, and that's where I met my late wife, which was a big bonus. I served there for a long period.

I started my working life as an accountant and worked through the nine counties of Ulster. In the 1970s I was approached – because I had an accounting background – to be a member of the Prince's Trust.

I served 23 years in the Prince's Trust and like most volunteers it became a priority in my life.

Eventually I became the local chair of the Trust. We gave money with the minimum of red tape – to individuals, groups and national organisations. For me the biggest payback was dealing with individual young people – sometimes as little as £25 made all the difference. '

Jim McDonald introducing Bill Osborne, Prince's Trust volunteer, to Prince Charles

From drab carpark to fab garden

By Maeve Connolly

HARD work and gallons of paint have turned a drab west Belfast parking area into a fun garden for disabled children. The sensory garden opened on Tuesday at the Divis Community Centre on the Falls Road thanks to the inspired work of the Prince's Trust – run by the Voluntary Service Belfast – and community organisation the Welcome Trust.

The Welcome Trust works with disabled people in west Belfast and hosts a twice-weekly after-school care programme as well as adult recreation evenings and entertainment for senior citizens.

The sensory garden has foliage such as apple trees, strawberry plants, thyme, lavender and mint as well as bright paintings of various cartoon characters on the walls.

There is also an impressive snakes and ladders board painted in a sheltered patio area with hanging baskets and summer seats to complete the scene.

Theresa Hanna of the Welcome Trust said the garden was now in the care of the children who used the centre.

"Some of the kids have restricted mobility but due to the lay out they can have access to the plants and everything

AT A GLANCE...

Volunteers have transformed a drab parking space into a fun sensory garden for the disabled in west Belfast.

else here," Ms Hanna said.

"It's brilliant because it's an outside play area which is safe and secure.

"We wanted to make it visually stimulating and let the children take responsibility of its upkeep."

Ms Hanna said that the children had seen the outlines for the paintings and had been waiting with great excitement for the finished product.

She added that the trust would like to see the council become more involved in future projects at the centre.

Maurice Girvan from the Prince's Trust said it had taken the team of 13 volunteers less than two weeks to complete their task.

"The challenge was to brighten it up and bring in some plants and natural materials and they have done a fantastic job.

"The team have been fund raising for this for a while now. They washed cars, packed groceries and held a pub quiz."

■ GROUND FORCE: Volunteers from the Prince's Trust in the sensory garden at Divis Community Centre   PICTURE: Bill Smyth

'May Seth was the driving force behind Youth Action. She was also on the British equivalent body – the National Association of Youth Clubs. She was at an event for it when she met a cousin of mine, Sarah Morrison, who was in business and politics. May asked her, "Do you know anyone who would be suitable for the Northern Ireland Association". My cousin put my name forward.

Hampton House by Billy Campbell

I joined what was at the time a small organisation. The average age of the board was quite high – I was the youngest member of the committee.

My contribution was to chair the AGM and going out and visiting clubs with May Seth. As the years went by it grew and grew and became more professional – a high profile organisation. It has a high turnover now, with many special projects.

I retired last year and my son succeeded me. There was a handover in 2007. He's now fully involved.

The amount of time I spent in the clubs was limited. I did a lot of contact work and helped with fundraising. Funding then was short. Now it's mainly special projects, with funding from EU sources and government.

The new building was opened last year by Princess Alexandra – near College Square and

The new Youth Action building. Photo: Rory Moore

opposite Inst in the centre of Belfast. It's a brand new modern building. We were able to fund it because May Seth had bought a small Victorian House for a modest sum of money – up the Glenmachan Road, at Knocknagoney. The house up there had its own grounds, and was adapted to be a residential training centre. It ran a regular programme of events there, but the conditions changed and the accommodation wasn't up to standard... so the property was sold for a substantial sum of money –around £3 million. This enabled us to contemplate the brand new building with a range of modern facilities. It even has a small theatre for amateur dramatics. It opened shortly after I retired and is going very well. It has a theatrical group – the Rainbow Group.

For many years the AGM was a major feature for me. It was an all day event, far from just formalities. There would be displays by affiliated clubs, music, theatres. It fulfilled a useful role. It was cross-community but has become more so now – that was back in the late sixties.

I was always a name at the top of the paper rather than actually hands on.

I would go to national Association events in England – and met people like Lulu and Toyah who assisted the Association.

Photo: Youth Action

club over 37 years. God knows what they would have been up to if the boxing club hadn't been here.

Boxing teaches discipline, it improves their health and fitness. Here you have to be a psychologist, a brother, a dad – you have to be so many different things but you can't walk away.

Some people say boxing can damage you – but football or any sport can damage you! We were once told we couldn't get a grant because boxing was a dangerous sport – that they were not giving money for one kid to hit another. Did they not know that boxing is one of the most protective sports going on in the country? It was the first sport to have a child protection policy.

I've made many good friends through this boxing club. I asked my friend Eddie to come and help out for two weeks – that was thirty four years ago. He's the treasurer of the club now. '

EDDIE O'NEILL *Ligoniel Boxing Club*

' I have never boxed a day in my life, but I said I'd help out for a few weeks. I joke that it was my biggest mistake – but we've been here through thick and thin.

When vandals raided the roof they took away £15 of lead – yet it caused thousands of pounds worth of damage. We had to use drums and plastic buckets to catch the rain, and then we had to empty these night after night. It was hard work.

The building was an old school that was out of use. We were left with a sinking boat; and we had to fight to keep it going. Many nights we were stopped by the Brits and the Paras: *'Who are you? Where are you going?'* That was a nightly occurrence, and the kids also had to go through that all the time. Yet through all the bombs and the shooting we kept the club open. It was either dedication or stupidity.

"When I started here I had hair! We always had a laugh – if we didn't, we wouldn't have survived. '

Exterior view of Ligoniel Boxing Club, in disrepair.
Photo: Sean McAuley

Ligoniel's Sean Magee wins Ulster Gaelic Games title

Ligoniel's ABC talented young boxer Sean Magee bounces back from a narrow defeat in the All-Ireland championships semi finals to add another title to his collection

CHAMPION: Ligoniel's Sean Magee is declared winner over Bernard Blair St Bronagh, Tyrone

STEWART McAFEE
Amalgamation of Northern Ireland Supporters Clubs

George Best and Martin O'Neil – NI v Iceland, Windsor Park 1978. Photo: Stanley Matchett

'Throughout 'the Troubles', the majority of Northern Ireland fans were proud of one truth: our international teams always contained players from both sides of our divided community, giving their all on the football field.

Ask any Northern Ireland fan to name their all time heroes, and you can be guaranteed that the list will include players from different sides of the religious/political divide.

These sentiments were epitomised perfectly on a balmy June night in Valencia in 1982 – An East Belfast Protestant (Billy Hamilton) crossed the ball which found a West Belfast Catholic (Gerry Armstrong) to score the winning goal against Spain, in what remains probably the "finest hour and a half, plus injury time" in our 128 year history.

During 'the Troubles', traits of conflict were also evident on the terraces during Northern Ireland games. Sectarian chanting was common among a vociferous minority of supporters.

Whilst there had been repeated cries by fans for this to stop, a 'friendly' game against Norway in February 2001 served as a catalyst for change. On this occasion, Neil Lennon, making his 36th appearance in a Northern Ireland shirt, had his every touch of the ball booed and jeered by a small section of bigots, professing to 'support' Northern Ireland. It was Neil's first appearance since signing to Glasgow Celtic.

I still recoil when I think of the deep sense of embarrassment, hurt, and anger I felt that night. I was disturbed that a minority of so called fans could bring such shame.

In recent times, the anger of fans who no longer want to be dragged through the gutter by bigots leeching onto our team, has transformed into the IFA's "Football For All" initiative.

The Amalgamation of Official Northern Ireland Supporters Clubs (AONISC), representing approximately 80 Clubs based throughout Northern Ireland and further afield, has worked in close partnership with the IFA's Community Relations team.

The AONISC's objective, in support of "Football For All", is to ensure that anyone who wants to support the Northern Ireland International team, can do so in an environment free from, sectarianism, racism, bigotry and intolerance.

Stewart with members from the Amalgamation of Northern Ireland Supporters Clubs

To that end, much work has been done by the AONISC. This work includes support for the "Sea of Green" initiative; development of new songs designed to replace the sectarian chants of the past; delivery of talks and workshops to community and youth groups; the development of a "Football For All" DVD, telling the story of the fans' journey of transition through the eyes of the fans themselves; and fostering the development of a 'self policing' concept at matches.

There is much more work to do. Some challenges lie ahead and must be faced, with bravery and confidence. The AONISC is guided by what we believe to be best for the future security and progression of our International football team.

With small steps and small victories on and off the pitch, the Northern Ireland team has the potential to help in the healing process in this little dot on the globe.

We have the potential to ostracise bigots, from both sides, who have plagued Northern Ireland supporters for too long. ❜❜

SEAN McGETTIGAN *Gaelic Games*

' How did Casement Park come about? In 1943 Antrim got to the all-Ireland at Croke park. They lost to Cork 5-16 to 4. We came home and asked ourselves 'what happened?' The team would be playing on the pitch at Corrigan Park, but when they got to a level pitch at Croke Park it was too fast. We had to do something about it.

In 1944 Corrigan Park was reconstructed. The Antrim '44 convention proposed a car park be constructed. A committee was set up, I was made chairman.

By 1945 the committee had put together £10,000 from subscriptions from vintners and publicans. There were bazaars at Corrigan Park Outdoor Weeks – it was pretty solid throughout 1946-7.

Corrigan Park wasn't a good venue for big county games – there were only two roads in. Seamus McFerran and Tom Crummey were walking up the Andersonstown Road one day and looked over the hedge. What they saw was amazing – a twenty foot drop, a marshy mess of ground where the river was. They had a talk to an architect called Danny McRandall and asked him could they mark a pitch there? They decided to make a go of it. We bought the land for £4,000 plus £160 ground rent. At that time – it was just after the Blitz of 1941 – there was plenty of landfill around. We built up the surrounds as it was a twenty foot drop.

To raise funds we created a 'pool'. The first year we collected £9,000. In 1948 we made £25,000. At one stage we had 210,000 subscribers from all over Ireland.

The pool was a success. It made £125,000 over the

> *I was chair of Antrim SCOR for thirty years; and SCOR secretary of the Ulster council for a few years – then I caught myself on.*

years. That was one shilling a week – which in those days was some money.

Side line seats were in vogue at the time, but I was against them. I was at the pictures one night and saw a soccer game in San Paolo. There was a moat of water round it. This is still the set up at Casement – the moat but with no water in it.

The stand ironwork was bought from an auctioneer in County Fermanagh – from a sale of American hangars which had been built at Lough Erne for the US planes to station during the war. It was bought for £4,500.

The stand was built and ready for opening on 10th June 1953. We also paid for ground on Shaw's Road – thirty acres. The ground was leased to three clubs. When we finished up after paying for everything we were free of debt, and still had £10,000.

Over the years we did bits and pieces of work on it. We had a paid secretary – everyone else was a volunteer. It cost us all money!

It opened on a Saturday and all the clubs took a section. It was a lovely day. They ran a relay from Thurles, where the GAA was formed, to bring up soil from Croke Park in an urn.

After that I took a rest – it had been ten years of very hard work – meetings every Thursday night, listening to everyone's story.

I got involved in Scor in Antrim – the entertainment days where all the clubs compete. I was chair of Antrim Scor for thirty years; and Scor secretary of the Ulster council for a few years – then I caught myself on.

During those years the GAA was not getting good publicity. It wasn't getting anything from the BBC.

In 1952 I was asked to do a GAA sports interview with the Head of Programmes. After two cups of tea he rang up the sports producer. Next night, I was sending in GAA results to the BBC. I've done that over the years – that's how much I'm retired.

For years I was in and out of the BBC. I used to do the Junior GAA on RTE – the Junior Sports magazine on radio with Jimmy McGee.

I'm 92 now and still sending in results to the BBC.

Sean McGettigan died in January 2010

GILLY McILHATTON *Gaelic Games*

'I've been involved most of my life in the GAA and played county hurling for Antrim. I joined the Club Mitchells at fourteen; by seventeen I was looking after the under 16 team, and at 18 was elected club secretary.

For thirty years I was involved in running Mitchells – as secretary, treasurer or chair. It started in the New Lodge Road in 1900, moved to the Falls in 1906 and in the sixties and seventies became the Andy town team. The pitch opened in Poleglass in 1988 and has been there since.

I got involved at country level – in 1974 I was asked to come as a selector for the senior hurling team. I was elected country team manager in 1977 until 1982.

I held various positions on the Antrim Hurling Board – chair, assistant secretary, committee member and chairman again.

Over the years I was gathering up club memorabilia. I had 250 pictures from 1902 to 2007, and wrote a club history which was actually published in 2008. Writing the history of the club was a big thing for me. I spent years in newspaper libraries. For the centenary year I gave a talk from memory – the history of the Mitchell club from 1900 to 2000.'

DAVID ELLIOTT *Templemore Swimming Club*

'Belfast City Council had to make cutbacks in its leisure budget and they said they could save money by closing Templemore.

Templemore was costing £350,000 each year, when there were other centres. They seemed to want to pick on Templemore – it was one of the easier ones to close.

Local residents and users of the pool were not happy. They contacted councillors and made a protest, outlining the reasons why it was wrong to close Templemore, especially in an area that's underprivileged. It was right in the middle of the Troubles. It would have polarised things even more if the centre closed. We took the case to the council, with the reasons why it should be kept open. We set up a committee and involved a range of people from different clubs and associations.

One of the first things was to come up with ideas to make sure the pool was more widely used. We started a competitive swimming club in November 1983 – we celebrated our 25th anniversary in November 2008.

The club is going from strength to strength. All the pool time is allocated – from 9am until 10pm – thirteen hours – Monday to Friday, with 98 per cent utilisation. It shows that there is a need for the pool.

There is both a recreational and learning aspect. We are able to further ability in water based sports like canoeing in the pool, and life saving. We are 'selling pool space' to lots of different clubs. Our income was guaranteed, with minimal staff input.

We provide teaching staff to schools. Community and competitive swimming clubs are the biggest user. Some clubs have a history going back to 1894 – the Queen's Island Ship Yard, the East Club, Neptune have long histories here and are still going.

All the voluntary input is by local people. The council gave us a lease on the building. In 1993 it became a limited company by the Templemore Users Trust – and is still run by that same number of people as directors.

The voluntary aspect is right across the spectrum of clubs, from competitive clubs – all run by volunteers to paid coaches who worked with the top ability kids. From the teaching to the management – it was all volunteers. Every club – from churches groups to other clubs – were run by volunteers.

The building needed a lot of work – it was an old Victorian building. It needed money – to add a fitness suite, to re-align the pool, the water filtration service had to be upgraded.

One of the aims of the Trust is to restore the building. It's starting to deteriorate. We need to get money to conserve the building for the city – a grade 2a listed building.

John Kirkwood. Photo: Rory Moore

One of the real heroes of the Templemore Swimming baths is John Kirkwood. He's in his nineties – and still takes part in dive-ins. He was the

BATHS BAN ON TEENY BIKINI TO STAY

Not an inch less, says committee

Article in Cityweek, 18 July 1968

While reiterating its "bikini-ban" the Baths Committee of the Belfast Corporation has agreed to allow girls to wear two-piece swimsuits in the four city pools at Templemore Avenue, Falls Road, the Grove and Ormeau Avenue. The difference between the two today is, in many cases, just over an inch of cloth.

Strangely enough, according to the Director of Public Baths, Mr. Robert Young, the policy declaration on — bikini or not — to bikini was brought about by tourists who visited the local baths and thought that they could 'wear the more skimpy swimsuit in Belfast pools. The locals, he claimed, did not seem to mind one way or the other.

The reason given for the ban on bikinis was that 80 per cent of the patrons at the four pools were 'children of school-age, decent sensible grown up children. And they want to be ... to look at something decent.

Twenty-year-old Anne Hunter would be asked to leave any of Belfast's four Council-owned swimming pools if she appeared in this bikini. Blue-eyed, blonde Anne was the first heat winner in the Miss TV contest and was an entrant in last night's Miss Portrush contest.

and sensible in the pool". "The bikini," said Mr. Young "was not meant for swimming in. Imagine someone diving into the water in one from the board at the Grove . . ."

While Mr. Young feels sure he and his superintendents — whose job it will be to discern between an inch too much showing and the right acreage — can tell the difference. But Cllr. Wesley Campbell, a member of the committee, admitted that he always thought the bikini was just a modern name for a two-piece.

"The baths is not the proper place for a bikini. It belongs on the beach," he claimed. "Anyway people go to these pools to swim, not to loaf around and show off their figures." Another member of the committee, Cllr. F. W. Watson said that the decision was only to "regularise things that were already happening. Could he tell the difference between the two? "I'm beyond worrying about it," he laughed.

The bikini-question started in 1953 and, with the exception of a temporary relaxation, has been in force since then. For a while last year several appeared at the Falls Road baths without arousing any undue comment but they, too, are now taboo. One argument which Mr. Young puts forward to strengthen his case is an event that brought stares and blushes in the Ormeau Avenue pool one Saturday last year. 'The pool was crowded. A girl was wearing a bikini. A fellow swam past. His toe caught the top of it. The girl was wearing half-a-bikini.'

The only woman member of the Baths Committee, Miss Irene McAlery, also found it hard to tell the difference. 'I am too old now to try to dictate to young people what they should wear. But as far as I can recollect at the last meeting we agreed to move with the times and allow these to be worn. They're two-piece aren't they?'

first coach of the swimming club. He is still teaching – a remarkable man. He was one of the best teachers – competition swimmers from all over wanted to be coached by him.

The competitive swimming club is very successful.

The first thing we did was to get more young people into the centre. It gives the kids somewhere to go, to have a sense of belonging, to learn to swim and to open them up to other sports like canoeing while improving their fitness levels and well being.

BOBBY MARTIN *Male Care Centre*

Bobby Martin enjoying a game of bowls

' In the streets, just off the Donegall Road, men would just stand around the corners, then when it rained, they would disappear into their houses. We wanted somewhere where men could call in, sit a while, play darts and dominoes, have a cup of tea and a sandwich.

This was back in the eighties. After a few weeks we started to get donations – someone might give you a TV, or a microwave, stuff for cooking with, toasters. Then as time went on we got some money, a suite of furniture and three tables.

This place provides some respite – away from

> *Men would just stand around in corners, then when it rained, they would disappear into their houses.*

their comfort zones. It's a place for men to sit and talk and do what they want. Pensioners will lend a hand to help other pensioners.

Highway to Health helps us make healthy dinners – meat, potatoes, vegetables and pudding. On a Friday you'll have 12 to 13 in here, and other pensioners – we bring the meals to them – we know then they get a healthy dinner.

Thousands and thousands of volunteer hours have gone into this place – there's about seven or eight people who put in a couple of hours every day.

This place is known all over – we travel all over Belfast – even during the troubles when the worst things were happening.

Pensioners come in here and they can tell some stories over a mug of tea and some biscuits. It's somewhere to go rather than sitting looking at the four walls or just watching TV. '

Bobby Martin died in September 2008.

MARJORIE JARDINE

' I was coming up to retirement and I said to the staff that I was thinking of volunteering. They looked at me like I was mad – they said, "Go home and sit with your feet up."

> *I said to the staff that I was thinking of volunteering. They looked at me like I was mad – they said 'Go home and sit with your feet up'.*

I retired on 3rd October 1993, and there was flowers and gifts, but I thought what do I do when the party's over? So I sat and did knitting and crocheting for six months, and thought this life is not for me, I'll just deteriorate silently and slip into a grave.

One day I walked up and down Donegal Pass and I kept looking towards the volunteer place. Eventually I walked up the steps and went in. I was given an interview and went on to do befriending. Over time you'd get to know the moods and the character of the person. Some pass on, some go into a home. At the moment I'm befriending a blind lady. She has a lot to give and I have learned a lot from her. '

Bid for older volunteers

By **MICHAEL MCCREADY**

AN EXCITING new resource to encourage older people to find out about volunteering opportunities in their local area was launched last week at the Voluntary Service Bureau.

"You'd be surprised what volunteering has to offer' is the message from the agency who are working in partnership with Northern Bank, Volunteer Bureaux Northern Ireland and the Department for Social Development.

Julie Cusick from Voluntary Service Bureau said: "Older volunteers not only bring a wealth of experience to volunteering roles, but they also get to try new things too.

"Volunteering is all about choice — people get involved because they want to and it is a great opportunity to try something new whilst making new friends, becoming

creditorial@belfasttelegraph.co.uk

more active or passing on experience.

"It is up to the individual how much time they can give. From as little as one hour a week, volunteering offers a host of opportunities and getting involved is simply a matter of calling your local volunteer bureau on the volunteering freephone 0800 052 2212."

David O'Donnell from Northern Bank said: "Older people are the theme for December during this, the Year of the Volunteer 2005. We want to celebrate all the older volunteers in our community and to encourage more to get involved.

"There is a volunteering role out there for everyone, from neighbourhood watch schemes to conservation work, from befriending to committee

member, from driving to mentoring.

"We want potential volunteers to think about what they want to do and then get involved."

The Year of the Volunteer is a UK-wide celebration of volunteering and voluntary activity which is co-ordinated by the Volunteer Development Agency in partnership with BBC Northern Ireland, Volunteer Bureaux Northern Ireland, Northern Bank and the Department for Social Development.

The campaign aims to raise the profile of volunteers and to encourage more people to find out about volunteering by calling their local volunteer bureau on freephone 0800 052 2212.

For information on the Year of the Volunteer, visit www.volunteering-ni.org.

● Northern Bank branch manager Gary King, Volunteer Service Bureau co-ordinator Lindsay Taylor and Lila Lamb, volunteer, enjoy a cuppa and a chat at the Voluntary Service Bureau.

MARION MAGUIRE *ChildLine*

' I do telephone counselling with ChildLine. I saw an advert for ChildLine looking for volunteers and they were doing a recruitment drive in Belfast.

I went along to an information evening, to find out more about the organisation. It allowed me to meet some of the other volunteers in ChildLine. I talked to them about their experience. I've always wanted to work with children, but with the career path I chose, unfortunately

> *Think of any child and any type of problem, we receive that through childline.*

working with children wasn't something I was involved in.

I found out what ChildLine would require from a volunteer, what commitment they were looking form a volunteer.

With ChildLine I look after calls from across Great Britain, from children and young people, on a wide range of different issues. It can be falling out with a friend, a tiff with a sibling, family relationship problems bullying, sexual abuse, physical abuse, suicide, runaways – the issues are endless. Think of any child and any type of problem, we receive that through ChildLine.

When I signed up I was very clear that I had the time to commit to them. I commit four hours a week; I can work it into my schedule.

I do voluntary work with a fantastic organisation that does a lot of good for children. I get a lot from it. ChildLine have committed a lot to me in terms of the ten week training programme. It was a good foundation for me; I hadn't previous experience of being a counsellor. It gave me the skills to be able to go on the phone and talk to children.

I feel very supported by the organisation. Obviously now I have the core skills in terms of counselling, I have a better understanding of some of the issues children have to deal with. '

Online volunteering with ChildLine

Volunteer to give your time helping children online and we'll give you all the support you need to do it. You can make all the difference.

www.nspcc.org.uk   **ChildLine**   NSPCC
Cruelty to children must stop. FULL STOP.

BILL MORROW
Retired Senior Volunteer Programme

' As a small child I was exposed to the ethos of doing things for other people – something that's now called voluntary work.

When I was eight – in 1939, I joined the cubs where we were taught to do at least one good job a day. I got involved in the scout messaging service – that was my contribution to the war effort!

As I got a bit older I was approached to be a scout leader. When I retired my contribution was acknowledged – I became vice president of the local scout association and now honorary secretary of the local scout council.

Volunteering was never a name put on it. In my formative years, I saw my mother involved in the Ulster Street Savings Scheme. She brought me up to see that people did things for other people.

I went into employment at Harland & Wolff for the next 40 something years, until there was a massive redundancy programme in the company in the mid-1980s.

Volunteer led projects such as Transport and Home Security enable older people to remain independent in the community. In 1999, 3 volunteers spent 1577 hours fitting 348 Security Devices and smoke alarms to 225 people living in the greater Belfast area. While 40 volunteer drivers spent 3447 hours providing transport which enabled older people to access hospital appointments, podiatry clinics, Day Centres and assistance with outings and shopping.

Bill Morrow fixing locks as a volunteer

At its peak in 1946 there was 24,000 on its payroll, when I left in 1989 it was 1,800.

Six of us were selected to be redundancy counsellors and were sent for training – which covered things like what should people put on their CVs, how would people answer the question: 'what have you been doing since you became redundant?' During the training we were told that voluntary work was one way of showing employers that you had been doing something.

My older daughter was connected with VSB. I heard her talk about it so I made contact and was asked to come in for a chat. They asked me what were my talents so I said I was useful with my hands. VSB had started its home security scheme, and they asked if I would be interested. I ended up doing that for the next fourteen years. It involved fitting home security items in old people's homes – locks for windows and doors, smoke alarms, other internal security devices. '

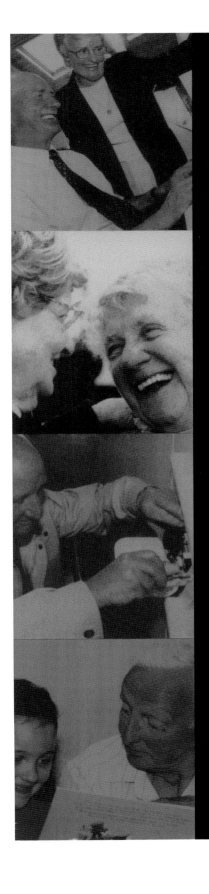

Third Age Volunteering

A Briefing Paper
by
Fiona Murray, BSc(Hons)

vsb

' I'd been a volunteer for approximately ten years before I realised that what I was doing was volunteering. My brother-in-law had bought an old church property and it needed a lot of work. So I'd volunteered every Tuesday night for ten years, working on this property, to try to get it into shape for youth groups. It is known as the Glebe.

Looking back I was very grateful for this project as I was able to learn a lot of skills like plumbing, tiling, electrical work, plastering, brick laying, tiling. I'd always been a keen DIY person.

When the project came to an end I was given early retirement at around the same time from the bank where I'd worked. I used to sit around the house, sometimes I'm sure I was just in the road. At this time my daughter was training to be a nurse and she'd come home every weekend and ask me what had I done that week. She'd say 'Have you not been to VSB to see if they can offer you something?'

So after much coercion, in late 1991 I phoned VSB. I said I was quite handy with most trades and so they asked if I'd like to do some woodwork. At that time VSB had a woodwork shop so I volunteered two days a week to build bird

> *I'd been a volunteer for approximately ten years before I realised that what I was doing was volunteering.*

boxes and bird tables – I didn't get the nickname the bird man of VSB for no good reason!

I enjoyed that time, but then the woodwork shop closed. Now, I had to find and do other things.

East Belfast Mission needed a minibus driver. Initially they said they were in a bit of a hole and needed someone for a short time. It turned out it must have been a very deep hole – because I was with them for the next four or five years.

At the time a new initiative was evolving – and that was the RSVP – the Retired and Senior Volunteer Programme.

The RSV Programme is something to look forward to. We do many different things like driving folks to hospital appointments or clinics. For some folk who are getting chemotherapy that lift is very much appreciated – the simple fact that they don't have to sit for ages in a hospital minibus after their ordeal.

Other folk I have taken to hospital for wheelchairs or walking sticks and things of that nature, having spent the last sixteen or seventeen years as a volunteer. I do hope that I will be able to continue with this for some time as I find it very therapeutic and it has helped me to enjoy my retirement. '

MONA McCONNELL *Volunteer Christmas Dinners*

I worked in social services from 1975 to 1990 – with the elderly, and with volunteers on Meals on Wheels. Throughout the year I saw a great need for contact on Christmas Day. There were a lot of vulnerable old people in North and West Belfast – some cases were shocking. They were so alone – with no one around to say 'Hello, how are you?' Christmas can be a very lonely time.

In 1975 I asked a number of volunteers would they help deliver meals I would make in my own home. It was not the meals that were important, but the contact. People don't want other people coming to their door out of pity – but if something is brought – you take away the indignity of their loneliness. In the first year we did 28 meals. Last year I still had some of those volunteers who served up the first meals.

From that first year in 1975, when we developed the service – it grew to 493 meals.

We used Parkmount Day Centre and covered

Belfast Christmas Lights. Photo: Stanley Matchett

> ### It gave Christmas back its meaning to them – a time of hope, celebration; a time of memories.

from the Shore Road, through North Belfast, to the Shankill Road. We developed a service for carers and deliverers. We had people playing piano and everyone got a cooked breakfast. As the meals were prepared to go out, the volunteers would catch up with people they hadn't seen all year. You could feel the heat and the warmth from those people.

The meals were sent out with small gifts that were donated. We'd do up the trays to make it look Christmassy. Sometimes the funds would dry up – but there was always something extra on the tray – even if it was only a couple of small oranges.

Our volunteers were a motley crew. Perhaps people for whom family life had broken down, through death or divorce or hard luck. It gave Christmas back its meaning to them – a time of hope, celebration; a time of memories. We developed a sit-in service in a day centre in Newington. There would be up to forty people there.

The recruitment of volunteers was by word of mouth. I don't know how some of them heard about it. Last year we had a lot of emigrants from all over the place. It gave them a day of companionship, of warmth.

There isn't a lot of time so what we endeavour to do is to keep the number of deliveries down for each volunteer – to a maximum of five meals. That gives them a chance to spend a little time with the person.

Things have changed for the better since 1975. Christmas changes for each of us as we get older. Families change, needs change, wants change.

JOAN McQUOID *Cruse Bereavement Care*

My earliest volunteering was as a Girl Guide leader in the late fifties and the sixties, then later in a fundraising group for the Save the Children.

In 1970 I did a course in adult literacy, and worked as a volunteer tutor to adults. I hadn't appreciated that so many people couldn't read well, or were dyslexic. This generated my interest – I was a psychologist and had always been interested in things like that.

In 1985 I did a counselling skills course at Queen's. Cruse was just starting up and the year I did the course, on the last day – it was announced that Cruse were looking for volunteers. I popped

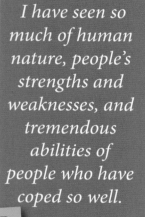

I have seen so much of human nature, people's strengths and weaknesses, and tremendous abilities of people who have coped so well.

along and said I was interested. I did a short course in bereavement counselling and early in 1986 became a volunteer with Cruse. Over the years I've been a committee member, a trainer, a supervisor, a counsellor. I feel I get an enormous amount back from doing this work. It's something I've enjoyed immensely, although it can be very exhausting.

Things have changed since the early days at Cruse in the 1980s, it's become much more professionalised. Cruse runs professional courses for its volunteers – very rigorous training.

All volunteers are trained in counselling skills, nowadays called Bereavement Support Volunteers – it's more than just befriending.

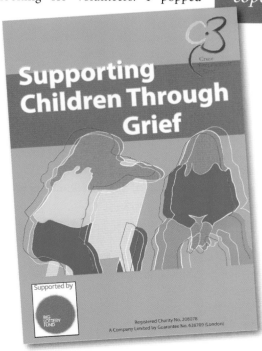

The counsellors have to also get supervision. I'm a trained supervisor – so I have to go to see a supervisor for supervisors! It's a big commitment. When I'm talking to my sister on the phone she'll say 'I suppose you'll be at Cruse again.' Sometimes I think 'what am I doing this for? But I get a lot out of it.

It's a job worth doing. It's rewarding to see the person's face change – to see them move from sitting slumped in the chair to becoming more confident, to look forward to their life ahead. There is no magic wand – life will be difficult, but they know they have a worthwhile life to live. It's not easy – but it's very, very worthwhile.

Through Cruse I can do something to help people in pain. I have seen so much of human nature, people's strengths and weaknesses, and tremendous abilities of people who have coped so well.

JESSICA HAMILL *HIV Support Centre*

'I'm Jessica Hammill and I first got involved with the HIV Support Centre two and a half years ago. I knew a few people with HIV. I went to the HIV Support Centre and saw the volunteers and the other people sitting there, and I thought it would be fun to be a volunteer. I help with fundraising for World Aids Day and the other events. Last year on the 1st December we released balloons from a big net. We let them go outside the City Hall. The Lord Mayor and Caroline Stewart and lots of other people who work at the HIV Support Centre were there.

Jesica Hamill on World Aids Day 2008

I go in to the HIV Support Centre every time with my uncle and just talk to people. I was practising my speech for World Aids Day. I was telling a story – about a girl who lives in Thailand and has lived all her life with HIV. Both parents had died – her name was Noo and she lived in North Thailand. She must have different medicines, she has to fetch her medicines herself and walks miles to get them; then she has to hide them in a bucket because her grandfather's an alcoholic and he will take them and spend the money on alcohol.

Being a volunteer makes you feel really good, helping people who are not as fortunate as you. It feels very nice, it gives you a boost.

Every time I go there I speak to people – people from all over the world of different colours and different religions, all ages and backgrounds.

Whenever I went back to school after World Aids Day people asked loads of questions – it was really cool.

I did an interview for Radio Ulster and had my picture in the Belfast Telegraph and Irish News.

There's another volunteer who's roughly my age, but I'm the youngest volunteer at the HIV Centre. They are young, old, people with dark skin and people with light.

The HIV Centre gives support and advice. People can get massages and complementary therapies, or free tests. We can tell them where to go for help, and there's a free helpline. It's important to help raise awareness – some people think you can get HIV from touching. They don't understand. I tell my friends at school about it.

Africa has a lot of HIV but it's a developing country so they don't have as many support centres. If anyone has HIV or if they want to volunteer, they can just drop in anytime or go on to the website or the free helpline. The first impression is that everyone is so optimistic, upbeat and happy.

Everyone in the HIV Centre who has HIV or comes down there is united, they stick up for each other. '

Jessica Hamill was 11 years old at the time of this interview

CONTRIBUTORS

Jonathan Bardon

Gerald Dawe

Richard Mills

Peter Rankin

Roy Snowden

Mike Maloney

Kevin McCavanagh

John Glendinning

Darren Ferguson

Jennie McCullough

John Kindness

Billy Campbell

Margaret Marshall

Patsy Harbinson

Stephen Harris

Jim McKeown

Fionnuala O'Connor

Ann McManus Irish News

Baroness May Blood

 Anne Walker

 Les Allanby

 Romana Khoury

 Barney McCaughey

 Sophie Bryson

 Gareth Lee

 Michael Hall

 Ann Collins

 Vincent Bent

 Mrs Khan

 Peter Emerson

 Billy Campbell

 Sir Kenneth Bloomfield

 Felicity McCartney

 Marie Abbott

 Kate Campbell

 Danae Kindness

 Maggie Andrews

 Pat Ryan

 Maggie Spence

 Wendy Osborne

Margaret Clinton

Auxiliary Bishop Donal McKeown

Ania Kostyszym

Geraldine Reid

Mary Francis Bradley

Duncan Morrow

Bill Logan

Owen Maguire

Leanne Donaghy

The Lord O'Neill of Shane's Castle

Jim McDonald

Joyce Murphy

Dorothy Agnew

Eddie O'Neill

Sean McAuley

Stewart McAfee

Sean McGettigan

Gilly McIlhatton

David Elliott

Bobby Martin

Marjorie Jardine

 Marion Maguire

 Bill Morrow

 Harry Press

 Mona McConnell

 Joan McQuoid

 Jessica Hamill

 Sydney Stewart

 Peter McLachlan

FINAL WORDS *Bill Osborne*

It is easy, and perhaps this is its inherent strength, to underestimate the value and impact of volunteering. The volunteering act is regularly only seen in the singular and not collective. These volunteer stories whilst of individuals, demonstrate the collective impact of single acts.

A G Grayling, in his book of essays, 'The Form of Things' informs us that "the average human life is less than a thousand months". This is reduced to a mere 600 months when time taken for sleep is discounted. Grayling concludes, "A lifetime is a truly fleeting thing". The gift of one's time is therefore a generous and precious commodity to give away. It is a gift too precious to be dismissed as an inconsequential transaction between a giver and a receiver. Whilst to volunteer is intrinsically an individual's decision, it is by implication a decision that makes a statement which has local community,

societal and political dimensions.

Martin Luther King Jnr in 1963 in his letter from Birmingham jail to his fellow clergymen, asked the following question: "So the question is not whether we will be extremists, but what kind of extremists will we be? Will we be extremists for hate or for love? Will we be extremists for preservation of injustice or the extension of justice?"

In many ways these stories of individuals living in the midst of a violent conflict reflect this socio-political dimension. Powerless to change the macro environment, they found or created the space through volunteering to be 'creative extremists', bringing an enduring message of hope through positive engagement rather than the negativity and despair of violent conflict. Their enduring legacy is the portrayal of volunteering as a creative, liberating and empowering process and one which is at the heart of a just society.